What People are Saying about
Finding Truth, Finding Health

The Healing method described here is simple, speedy, and best of all sticky. I've trained in a number of healing modalities and found nothing as effective as HeartMind Healing. I am in awe of what I accomplished as a Student Practitioner of Rita's teaching. The training is like a PhD in energy healing. —Jennifer Keyes, USA (First HeartMind Healing Academy Graduate)

This work is the Quintessential Healers Bible. —Tanya Collop, Soul Coach, South Africa

Darkness feeds upon our fears. Darkness cannot drive out darkness; only Light can do that. Rita taught me how to let the Light within conquer the darkness of ignorance, allowing me to shine as my true self. —Radu Beleca PhD, Germany

Rita is truly an inspirational teacher and facilitator. I healed, discovered my true essence, and empowered myself. Her knowledge patience and compassion allowed for multi-faceted growth within a wonderful safe space. —Kasia Wojcik, Life Coach and Feng Shui Consultant, USA

Healings best kept secret is finally revealed. —Mullerie Rabe-Taljaard, South Africa

When Rita is assisting me let go I can feel the issue energetically move and then release. Even stuff I've been forever hiding from myself moves out. —Colleen Koltick, New York

I want to again offer my deepest gratitude to you for the very powerful session. I really, really enjoyed it immensely. Thank you for your open

heart, compassion and love. I feel so much stronger and clear and positive. I have said it before, but allow me to say it again—I am thankful for you in my life. I really am. You are a great Teacher! A great Healer.
—Ronell Zondo, Practising Sangoma, South Africa

FINDING
TRUTH
FINDING
HEALTH

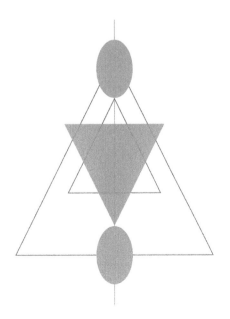

FINDING TRUTH FINDING HEALTH

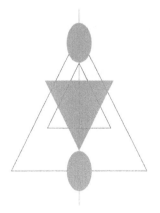

Rita Marr MPNLP., CCHyp

Teacup image on page 14 by Stux- Creative Commons CCO.
https://pixabay.com/photos/cup-saucer-tee-japanese-porcelain-188855/

Male & Female Spiral Vortices image on page 45 courtesy of The University of Science and Philosophy..www.Philosophy.org.

Tornado image on page 47 courtesy of Creative Commons CCO.

Gyroscope image on page 48 Creative Commons CCO.
https://commons.wikimedia.org/wiki/File:EmiMa-043.jpg.

Cell image on page 64 copyright: *The Inner Life of the Cell* movie, produced by XVIVO for Harvard University. Gratitude to Alain Viel for permission.

Water crystal images on page 72 copyright Masuro Emoto with thanks.

Image on page 73 copyright Sadia Chand used with permission from Rasmus Gaupp Studio Austria. Photo taken by AQUAQUINTA e.U.

Maypole image on page 118 copyright wikimedia.org/wiki/User:Jengod.

Second maypole image on page 118 copyright http://www.ifferjenn.com/tag/maypole/.

Gift box image on page 123 designed by
Racool_studio and used under Freepik Premium License.

It happened on purpose image on page 124 copyright Paul Roy www.paulroy.ca.

Cover design by Ivica Jandrijevic
Interior layout and design by www.writingnights.org
Book preparation by Chad Robertson
Illustrations digitized by Illumineer Media & Design
www.illumineermediadesign.com

ISBN: 978-1-7772273-0-2
LIBRARY OF CONGRESS CATALOGING-IN-PUBLICATION DATA:
NAMES: Marr, Rita., author
TITLE: Finding Truth, Finding Health– Toroids and Hara Lines – A Master Class for Healers and Lightworkers / Rita Marr CCHyp.,MPNLP
DESCRIPTION: Independently Published, 2020
IDENTIFIERS: ISBN 9781777227302 (Perfect bound) |
SUBJECTS: | Non-Fiction | Hara | Healing | Enlightenment |
CLASSIFICATION: Pending
LC record pending

Independently Published
Printed in the United States of America.
Printed on acid-free paper.

24   23   22   21   20   8   7   6   5   4   3   2   1

For Tanya Lee Collop
Whose psychic vision and artistic skill
described some of the energy illustrations
needed for this book.
Tanya consistently accompanies me on the research trail
as companion and delightful fellow traveler.

And
To You Dear Reader,
Kindred Spirit, and Lightworker

Blessed are the humans who look for the unseen things that
are intuitive
but not yet accepted in the reality of life,
for they will be rewarded with knowledge and wisdom
so that they will become the fore-runners
of the newest sciences on the planet.
— ANON

CONTENTS

LIST OF FIGURES

PREFACE

Gratitude to my unseen teachers

Gratitude is an energy that sets the stage for healing.
As you give so shall you receive.
As you receive so shall you give.

I wish to share with you more about the function and nature of the Human Electrical Energy System, specifically Toroids and Hara Lines. Why we need fully functional hara lines, what they do for us, how they work, how they affect us when they are dysfunctional and how our evolution is supported by being 'Harically aligned.'

Eastern Spiritual Teachers, especially in the martial arts context, have always understood the importance of the Hara level of our energetics. In the Western context of healing or body work little has been known about the Hara except through the work of Diane Stein and Barbara Brennan, both of whom I wish to thank for arousing my curiosity in 2005. I am about to share channeled knowledge that I was given in 2016.

Spirit Guides—I came to know them as The Council of Truth—were my teachers. I will be forever grateful that they initiated contact with me via Sally Reid, a psychic who has the ability to connect into a Stream of Consciousness from the Eternal One. Sally was kind enough to be the mouthpiece for a portion of this profound teaching.

An increasing number of Light workers are becoming curious about Toroidal fields and Hara lines which are a powerful, intrinsic part of our energy system. If you already know that it is possible to correct the movement of energy, if you have developed pure unadulterated perception, plus you have an enhanced connection with others, the Earth and the metaphysical realms, this book is for you.

ACKNOWLEDGEMENTS

My consciousness 'woke up' in 1991 and as a consequence I have voraciously read hundreds of books on the subject of metaphysics, estotericism and healing, attended a myriad of workshops and training courses. They are too numerous to mention. However, I have listed a number of particular books in Bibliography.

I would however like to say a great thank you to Sanaya Roman and Duane Packer for their channeling of Orin and Da Ben's method of *Awakening Your Light Body*. A six-month process that changed my life in 1995 so much so that I became a Teacher of their method.

I acknowledge also the teachings of Neuro Linguistic Programming and Hypnotherapy particularly in the form of the amazing work of rogue Psychiatrist Milton H. Erickson.

In addition, I send my gratitude to Coby Zvickler for his amazing *Empower Disc* method, the *Huna Teachings* of Tad James, *Emotion*

Code, Heart Math, and *EFT.* The *I Ching, TCM, Vedanta, Ayurveda, Human Design,* and Rudolph Steiner's teachings through the Anthroposophical Society. *Theosophy, Aromatherapy* and *Kinesiology,* particularly Ann Banks for her work with *Visual Remedies* and her excellent teaching methods for Dowsers, the late Michael Mann, and Pauline Turner for teaching me dowsing skills in 1992. Veronica Williams for opening my eyes to energy healing through Reflexology treatments in 1991. Plus, Barbara A. Brennan and Diane Stein for their preliminary work on the Hara. I thank the late Itzhak Bentov together with his widow Mirtala, who shared his work posthumously. His illustration of the Cosmic Egg began a search in me that has lasted years, and in many ways has culminated in the writing of this book (see video link in Glossary). Dagmar Wijnen my friend and soul mate who transitioned in 2017 is sorely missed. I am grateful for the research and studying we did together, and for her many channeled healing symbols, one of which I have used as an aid for Haric Alignment, and the other as an aid to connecting with the Higher Self.

There were many and varied methods I was exposed to that I used as steppingstones. I built on some bits and pieces of these methods and integrated the very special and unique channeled teachings from the Council of Truth through Sally Reid, more easily because of my background experience. I am indebted to all my clients and students for the trust they afforded me and the opportunities for expansion they offered me.

I am particularly grateful to the late Dr. David R Hawkins for his *Map of Consciousness* which is mentioned in Chapter Six.

INTRODUCTION

Humans are only inhibited they are never broken.
They just need assistance to help them uncover
the fullness of life and relieve the impediments.
— The Council of Truth

THE PURPOSE OF THIS BOOK is to inform and enlighten healers, light workers, life coaches, therapists, counselors, and those interested in gaining a deeper understanding of the nature of disease, and the role energy plays in health and wellness. I share this in the hope that you will then be better equipped to help yourself and your clients get more profound results quicker and more easily. I will endeavor to help you understand the nature of the mind in more detail, the mind body connection, the way energy flows both within and without the body, the multidimensional nature of the body, plus how to reconnect with our intrinsic healing abilities.

Humans generally are out of sync with themselves, their environments, and natural systems. Indeed, very few are in sync. We know that becoming in sync is required because the human body is a self-regulating organism and is therefore programmed to naturally find balance and heal itself, a state known as homeostasis. I'm sure you have realized that often pain or discomfort is a message that it's time to harness your own healing resources because the cure lies within you. My intention here is to introduce you to some techniques and concepts that may be new to you so you may have a deeper and broader understanding of our multi-dimensional metaphysical nature. These teachings are being introduced, or more accurately some aspects are being re-introduced after thousands of years of being forgotten, to create harmony between the energies of the individual in relation to each other and in relation to the Earth.

I hope that when you work with your clients to assist them to find their health, the information you learn here will help you awaken them to truth. If you help them find truth, they will find health.

All journeys begin with two questions:

Where are you now?
Where do you want to go?

The steps of the journey will be explained and backed up with proven research. Some of the information came as a consciousness stream from the Universal Mind, some comes from ancient teachings and word of mouth guidelines passed down from teacher to student through the ages. I will be quoting from some of the most trusted and professional sources such as Scientists, Doctors, University Professors, famous Authors, Universal Physicists and Researchers. Essentially with the help of Spirit Guidance and information downloaded from the collective Universal consciousness I have created a simple method of getting unstuck anywhere in life whether that be originating on a physical, emotional, mental, or spiritual level. I will be explaining why my method works, what it is, and covering some aspects of how it works. If healers and light workers want to emulate and practice my method, then further training is required. This is available through online training courses, webinars, members only sites and a Practitioner Manual. I use ancient wisdom to solve contemporary problems.

One of my Students who is a well-qualified healer said to me: "My goodness this technique is amazing. If I compare it to my own healing work, I feel like I've been sewing on buttons, while you, on the other hand, do major surgery."

Online Training Courses

Master Classes and Practitioner Training:

www.heartmindhealingacademy.com

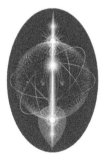

PROLOGUE

Any sufficiently advanced technology
is indistinguishable from magic.
— ARTHUR C. CLARKE

Charles Fort also pointed this out in his book *Wild Talents*: "...a performance that may one day be considered understandable, but that, in these primitive times, so transcends what is said to be the known, that it is what I mean by magic."

It is said that we have control over only three things:

Our Attitude
Our Emotions
Our Energy

If I was to have to choose control over only one of these I would choose control over my energy, because I believe if we have control over our energy we automatically have control of our emotions and attitude of mind. This book is for you if you would you like to learn how to effectively control your energy.

We are able to release issues as energy because we have within us a natural energy re-cycling plant. It is a little known fact that we are born with the ability to change our physical, emotional and mental well-being on-demand. As with all other abilities though, we need to learn how to hone the skill so we become adept.

My intention is to both explain the nature of our energetic being and then expose you to how to become adept at change on-demand by skillfully using your inner re-cycling plant.

I've learned over the years never to reject an idea simply because it seemed miraculous. Miracles are simply occurrences that cannot be explained from a present perspective. However, take a different perspective and the miracle seems simply explained or easily understood. Watch a magician work from the perspective of the audience, then watch him work from the perspective of backstage. Will you see a different perspective of his trick?

I have respect for that which transcends my current understanding. Often I just need to question, get curious, or look from a different perspective, in order to grasp the truth of a new challenging idea. Remember a cube has six sides and each may be decorated differently which may create an illusion of looking at six different objects.

I know of no way to force anyone to believe anything they may not want to believe. I will present compelling evidence in the hope of inspiring you to be curious and seek more to make the unknown, known and understood.

When we are learning something new we all go through the following stages:

Confusion

Uncertainty

Understanding

Certainty

Peace

Everyone seeks peace as an innate goal so we organically meet challenges in order to get there. If we truly want peace and we avoid challenge, then we will never achieve it. Simple.

CHAPTER 1
FINDING TRUTH

All truth passes through three stages.
First, it is ridiculed.
Second, it is violently opposed.
Third, it is accepted as being self-evident.
— ARTHUR SCHOPENHAUER 1788-1860

T IS SO IMPORTANT that we have an open mind. Curiosity serves us well. We need to engender the attitude of relying more on our feelings than on our thoughts. The first time I became conscious of my own energy it was a feeling. I trusted this reaction because it was related to a physical sense. Our feeling sense can act as our bridge into the more metaphysical experiences. Meta means 'outside of' therefore metaphysical means outside of the 'physical' reality we have learned to perceive. Our senses perceive effects. I strive to discover causes. The cause of a physical effect is often metaphysical. True knowledge is the understanding of cause whether it be metaphysical or physical. Empirical observation and experimentation is often invalid because it ignores cause.

Confusion precedes a higher level of order. Confusion always comes during the process of learning new things. Debate loosens limiting belief systems. Let the love in this book carry you gently forward. As you read please just consider the possibilities of 'what if this is true?'

There are many examples which are evidence that we can achieve 'only what we believe we can achieve.' I remember swimming lessons with my father. As I left the deep end of the pool, to swim the full length to the shallow end for the first time, he said, 'you just have to believe you can do it.' And do it I did! The whole way I just kept telling myself I could do it. Over and over again I said it. What a feeling of achievement!

Roger Bannister set the record for running a mile in under four minutes in 1954. His time was a record breaking three minutes 59.4 seconds on 6th May of that year. Until then no one believed it could be done. Amazingly the record was broken forty-six days later by John Landy whose time was 3.57.9. Then an even shorter time of 3.47 was achieved by the Yugoslav runner Otenhajmer. Since 1999 the record has stood at 3.43.13 achieved by Hichan El Guerrouj of Morocco.

The Mind

A calm mind is much more resourceful than a troubled or busy mind. A calm mind enables us to perceive differently. Pure perception requires a calm mind.

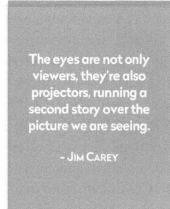

The eyes are not only viewers, they're also projectors, running a second story over the picture we are seeing.

– JIM CAREY

How the Mind Works/How Trauma Occurs

Most of us perceive in a distorted way, like a selective camera lens. Through either rose colored glasses, or dark grey colored glasses. The filters inside our minds cause us to skew what we perceive. We have inbuilt cognitive screens. An example would be: do we live life as if the glass is half empty or half full? These filters are created as a result of our experiences. Beliefs create filters. If we believe we are victims of a harsh world, then we will only perceive evidence of that belief. If, on the other hand, we believe we are lucky, then we are.

We automatically prove our beliefs to be valid by choosing what we perceive. We can keep ourselves trapped in the matrix of our own minds. An example would be seeing an outfit in a store for the 'first time', then buying it because it was different to anything we had ever seen before. After we bring it into our world, only then do we notice other's wearing the same outfit.

NLP¹ Communications Model

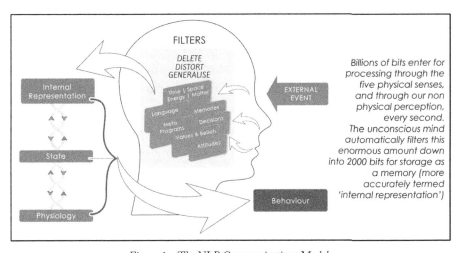

Figure 1 - The NLP Communications Model.

Every second we receive many billion bits of information into our minds via our five senses. This is shown on figure 1 as the 'External Event.' This enormous amount of information is too much to process. We have to reduce it down, to just two thousand bits, by automatically filtering out what we are disinterested in, at that precise second. The filters we use for this are created over time as a result of conditioning and experience. Most of them during the first two years of life when we are so trusting and innocent, we absorb sponge-like, the beliefs, attitudes, cultural mores and values of role models and those who care for us. We 'program' ourselves unknowingly and those programs, unless changed, will dominate our life experience. Plato cautioned, "Do not train a child to learn by force or harshness; but direct them to it by what amuses their minds, so that you may be better able to discover with accuracy the peculiar bent of the genius of each."

When we experience an event and create a memory, an internal representation of the event, that memory is made from a tiny amount of the original information. This explains how two people can never have exactly the same response to an event. Witness statements vary. The grey or the rose-colored lenses are at work within the filters.

The memory/perception/internal representation creates the 'state' (emotional, mental) in which we find ourselves and that dictates how our body (physiology) responds. Whether that be head held high or head bowed low. Tense shoulders or relaxed ones. A strong peristaltic wave in the intestine because we are relaxed or a sluggish one, because of anxiety and tension.

The memory, together with the state, plus the physiology, create our behavior. Therefore, if we wish to change any of our behaviors, then we need to change our perception. To change our perception we need to change the way filters operate. This book explains the process of changing the filter's operation at will so that you can make informed choices about how to behave moment to moment. Yes, it's that simple. All that's needed is trust in the process, then to take action. It is only then that you are able take your power back.

Perception

The colloquial saying "just look at it this way" reframes perception.

Art appreciation is a good example of unique personal perception. A creation one person finds beautiful or attractive, another may find distasteful or abhorrent. When each person views these artistic creations, they react differently at the emotional level. Same stimulus, different response.

The ultimate goal of perception is to perceive our personal individual truth. Every human being is in search of this.

We can all choose to correct the movement of erroneous or debilitating perceptions and misapprehensions. We can unstick an old perception.

Perception is projection. It may take a moment to appreciate what that means. Things that are coming at you are actually coming from you. You only hear what you want to hear. See what you want to see. You created the world you are perceiving.

Dr. David Hawkins in his book *Letting Go: The Pathway of Surrender* said it well, "The other person merely mirrors back what we are projecting onto them." The Universal 'Law of Return' refers.

Beliefs

A belief is causal to experience. Beliefs have power over us. Limiting beliefs exert power, as do empowering beliefs. There are 150,000 receptors in each cell that work on a mental, emotional, and physical level. A Limiting Belief can change the cells function immediately from function to dysfunction. The converse is also true. Release a limiting belief, install an empowering belief in its place, the cell is then able to function optimally once again.

Energy

It is now a proven scientific fact that matter per se does not exist. Everything consists of a specific frequency of vibration.

Energy, Vibration, Resonance, Electricity

One of the first concepts we all grapple with when attempting to understand the metaphysical[2] nature of our world is that everything is energy or vibration. We

> Physicists abandoned their belief in a Newtonian material universe because they had come to realize that the universe is not made of matter suspended in empty space but energy.
>
> – BRUCE H LIPTON

wonder how can that be when our body, the chair we are sitting in seems so densely physically present. How could the chair, the book we happen to be reading at the time, the feelings we had, the beliefs we held, the behavior patterns we used, the body we live in, be just vibrating energy with negligible matter present? It's difficult to grasp with the Newtonian based scientific education the majority of us were exposed to up until the recent popularity of Quantum Physics Theories.

We accept that sound, music, and words are vibration. This is why we are affected so profoundly by a beautiful piece of music or a loud unpleasant noise. In the old days of the silent movies the pianist had to create the 'mood' in the audience to emotionally match what was happening on screen by playing appropriate music. The soundtrack of movies performs the same function today.

Sound creates form. Evidenced by the visual patterns of Cymatics.[3]

Resonance

Resonance is a feature of healing and paranormal sensing.

We often hear people say that 'resonates with me.' Indeed, I say it myself. I started to think about resonance in the context of humans. I came across this story of how resonance can be used in everyday life. I loved it enough to want to share....

Charles Hirschberg, the Science News Editor for *Popular Science* magazine shares a simple experience that taught him about how science integrates into everyone's every-day life.

"One of my mother's earliest memories is of standing in her crib at the age of about 2, yanking on her 11-year-old brother's hair. This brother, her only sibling, was none other than Richard Feynman, destined to become one of the greatest theoretical physicists of his generation: enfant terrible of the Manhattan Project, pioneer of quantum electrodynamics, father of nanotechnology, winner of the Nobel Prize, and so on. At the time, he was training his sister to solve simple math problems and rewarding each correct answer by letting her tug on his hair while he made faces. When he wasn't doing that, he was often seen wandering around Far Rockaway, New York, with a screwdriver in his pocket, repairing radios.......at age 11, mind you.

My mother taught me about resonances when I was about 12. After more than four decades of geophysical research, my mother, Joan Feynman, is getting ready to retire as a senior scientist at NASA's Jet Propulsion Laboratory.

She is probably best known for developing a statistical model to calculate the number of high-energy particles likely to hit a spacecraft over its lifetime and for her method of predicting sun spot cycles. Both are used by scientists worldwide.

Anyway back to resonances: We were on a camping trip and needed wood for a fire.

Together with my brother and sister, I looked everywhere, without luck. Mom spotted a dead branch up on a tree. She walked up to the trunk then shook it.

"Look closely," she told us, pointing up at the branches. "Each branch waves at a different frequency." We could see that she was right. So what? "Watch the dead branch," she went on. "If we shake the tree trunk in just the right rhythm, we can match its frequency and it'll drop off." Soon we were roasting marshmallows."

In the last twenty plus years I have come to understand that 'matter' does not exist, even though we believe our senses when we see 'solid objects', there is only vibrating energy. Universal Physics is the study of the basic principles that govern the physical world around us. Are you ready to be fast tracked through a steep learning curve? I need to expand on this concept a little more. There follows some simple examples, or quotes, from some of the most amazingly profound research studies and experiments. Physicists and Metaphysicists who have spent their lives exploring the realm of the unseen, yet non-the-less real.

Science, until recently, promoted the idea that if you cannot see it or measure it, it didn't exist. When in fact many unseen and unfelt by some, but not others, things do exist.

Let's consider the historical facts. First there was Isaac Newton three hundred years ago who formed the Newtonian model of physics which postulated a mechanical universe. Newton's *'Laws of Motion'* are three physical laws[4] that formed the foundation for what's known as *'Classical Mechanics.'* They describe the relationship between a body, the forces acting upon it, and its motion in response to those forces.

Isaac Newton published these laws in *Mathematical Principles of Natural Philosophy* in 1687. Newton used them to both explain and investigate the motion of many physical objects and systems. Newton's law has since been superseded by Einstein's theory of general relativity.

Figure 2 - There is enough energy inside the space in this empty cup to boil all the oceans of the world.

The old archaic electrical engineering model was formed over 127 years ago yet the present scientific establishment adamantly refuses to correct the sadly flawed classical electrodynamics model even though 1916, 1945, 1968, 1973, 1984 and 1995 were important years in the research of Quantum Physics which proved the model was flawed. Today it is time for us to accept what the Quantum World offers us in the form of alternative energy to fossil fuels, healing, and growth.

Tom Bearden,[5] has done some sterling work which is useful in understanding how we can have energy[6] that does not involve raping the planet, mining coal, drilling or fracking for oil, drilling for gas and creating an ecological disaster in the process of extracting energy that must be processed giving rise to waste products which further toxify the environment.

There is enough energy inside the space in this empty cup (Figure 2) to boil all the oceans of the world. This is a fact well known in the scientific community. It was, for example, a favorite quote of Nobel Prize winning physicist Richard Feynman.[7]

I really enjoyed Bruce Lipton's explanation in *The Biology of Belief.*[8] He said "Quantum physicists discovered that physical atoms are made up of vortices of energy that are constantly spinning and vibrating; each atom is like a wobbly spinning top that radiates energy. Because each atom has its own specific energy signature or wobble, assemblies of atoms collectively radiate their own identifying energy patterns."

Dr. Lipton continued "Every material structure in the universe, including you and me, radiates a unique energy signature. If it were theoretically possible to observe the composition of an actual atom with a microscope, what would we see? Imagine a swirling dust devil cutting across the desert's floor. Now remove the sand and dirt from the funnel cloud. What you have left is an invisible, tornado-like vortex. A number of infinitesimally small, dust-devil–like energy vortices collectively make up the structure of the atom. From far away, the atom would likely appear as a blurry sphere. As its structure came nearer to focus, the atom would become less clear and less distinct. As the surface of the atom drew near, it would disappear. You would see nothing. In fact, as you focused through the entire structure of the atom, all you would observe is a physical void. The atom has no physical structure; the emperor has no clothes."

> The Universe is one dynamic whole in which energy and matter are so deeply entangled it is impossible to consider them as independent elements.
>
> – BRUCE LIPTON

I remember the erroneous atomic models of yesteryear, the ones with little balls orbiting a central core. How wrong they were. Compare these old visuals with a picture of nothing, which is more accurate because atoms are comprised of invisible energy not tangible matter!

All matter arises out of energy. To be precise electrical energy.

Resonance and Goal Setting

If you put your attention on something wonderful that you wish to receive, it is vital that you are vibrating at the same high rate as your goal in order to draw it to you. Plus, you need to be willing to receive it as it flows to you.

The most common hurdle to goal achievement is an existing low vibration within you, counteracting the high vibration of the goal, plus unwillingness, because of feelings of not being good enough, to receive what you could create. This is the real meaning of like attracts like. High vibrations attract high vibrations and low vibrations attract low ones.

In NLP we use the term 'towards' or 'away from' to describe this conflict. For example, do you want a better job because you are worried about not having enough money? Whenever you put your attention on the better job (high vibe) then you remind yourself of your fears of not having enough money (low vibe) therefore the motivation is 'away from' lack of money which is a low vibration. Wanting a better job may be a high vibration but will be undermined by the low one. All goals should be 'towards' motivated. For example, 'I want a better job so I can move to an off-grid home in nature where I will enjoy the natural high vibration of trees and grass every day', would be a better way of creating motivation.

We Are Electrical Creatures
What we experience as sound, as light or as emotion, is frequency.

Vibration and Energy in Relation to the Body
Every living thing is encased in an electrically charged field. When another electrically charged field comes into contact, or is introduced, a reaction occurs.

Our electrical field is influenced by the changing forces of the Earth, the cosmos, together with biomagnetic (from other living beings) and electromagnetic (from electrical equipment) forces. A healing Intention creates an electrical impulse or charge which when purposefully directed towards self or another living organism interacts with the electrical fields.

Human bodies are simply electrical equipment consisting of an input mechanism, storage battery, generator, and output mechanism.

Electricity is inherent in us and can be felt or observed easily. Have you ever felt what is termed a 'static electric shock' from a car door or from polyester clothing?

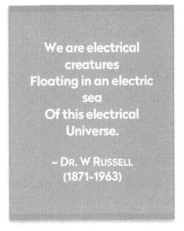

We are electrical creatures
Floating in an electric sea
Of this electrical Universe.

– DR. W RUSSELL
(1871-1963)

Being an astrological air sign, I have a lot of air in my system. In the cold, low humidity winter in Canada I get static electric shocks on a very regular basis. Those with more water, earth or fire may not get as many but we all experience them from time to time. Because we are electrical in nature we need to be 'earthed' just like any other electrical system, in order to function well.

As we learned from the marshmallow toasting story all living things have a unique vibration. The Sun, the Moon, rocks, trees, mammals, birds, fish, even bacteria, viruses, and plants. This is proven by the way sharks hunt their prey. They are sensitive to vibration in the water. They pick up the electrical impulses emitted by fish and all marine organisms, or indeed all living things.

In all creatures, including humans, there is a specific level of vibration that supports optimal health.

Discord is when a vibration is in disharmony, conflict, or disunity. There is an impedance of energy flow. Energy MUST flow. If it stops then its bad. Problems develop. For example, when the energy of money stops flowing life becomes difficult. Things need to flow, to move. Impedances create a 'dam.' Stuckness, stagnancy or discord results. There are an incredibly large number of factors that cause impedance of flow in humans. We will explore them later. Equally there are keys to optimum health which we will be exploring further. To regain a healthy state a vibrational balance within us needs to occur.

Be aware that ingesting or inhaling, for example, poisons, toxins, industrial chemicals, pesticides, herbicides, or domestic cleaning materials, changes our vibration and causes stress.

The low vibration of the toxin brings our energy down. Higher vibrations cause us to feel joyous. Lower vibrations create unhealthy, unhappy feelings.

Spirit Gives Rise to Physical Matter

I feel it's worth repeating. All things are created in spirit before they are physical.

Energetic Flow

In the Universe energy flows in a spiraling, water-like manner. Think about it: Water flows. The way water flows, or where it flows, has no meaning.

Therefore, it follows, that we should not ascribe meaning to where, or how, energy flows. No one ascribes meaning to the way water flows. Energy just moves and flows. That's it. It needs no rituals in order to flow or move. When water is stagnant it deteriorates. It ceases to be healthy. It's neither fresh nor potable. Energy is just like water in that it flows. We can make water flow through manmade channels. We can direct it by building canals or drainage ditches. Energy can also be directed. However, all that is required in order for energy to be directed, is intention. This is a very important point which needs repeating. Energy can be directed within the body using clear, positive intention.

Non Judgment

Judgments must cease if you wish to experience good health. In the world of energy there are no judgments. Just as in a computer there are no judgments; there is just 1 or 0. There are no mythologies around 1 and 0. Optimizing energetic flow thereby helping everyone to live more gracefully is my intention.

Self-responsibility

It's a really good idea to let go of victim mentality. I strongly recommend you help your clients to stop asking: 'Why me?' 'Why now?'

Suggest they ask instead 'I wonder what this is here to teach me?' 'What am I to learn from this?' Realize that we are responsible for creating everything we experience, good, bad, or indifferent. We must stop ascribing reasons or looking for something or someone to blame. Stop the whole 'she or he is the problem' narrative.

By way of example during the channeling session on this topic Sally was shown a life in 375BC where she was an eleven-year-old child meditating with a group of young Buddhist men in a Northern Indian school. A Hoard of Marauders came upon them and murdered them all. They offered no resistance. Firstly, the marauders were filled with glee at what they had done. Soon however that turned to remorse and shame.

The deaths, which at first could have been seen as purposeless, the question 'why' perhaps being asked fruitlessly, turned out to have a purpose. It was a flow. The dead agreed to use their lives as a teaching tool. Sally commented later that after tapping into that life, she felt satisfied with it. A lot of her past lives had ended early and she had come to realize that there was purpose to every single one.

It's worth repeating that the human body is both a great big receiver, generator, battery and transmitter of electricity.

Energy Just Wants to Flow

Energy flows through the human body in a figure of eight configuration (Figure 3). It crosses in the midpoint just below the belly button. This explains why a knee problem can cause a shoulder issue, or vice versa.

When we use our intention to create the rules of energetic flow, and tell the energy where and how to flow, we must specify how we want it to react to suit the needs of the individual. Imagine an irrigation system or an electrical grid where rules apply to movement. Just like the rules of the road ensure ease of traffic movement. When there is road work another route is found for the traffic to continue flowing. It's the same in the energetic flows of the body.

Getting energy unstuck, removing energetic blocks, together with ensuring energetic flow, is the key to health.

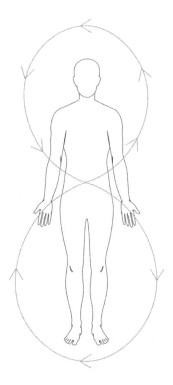

Figure 3 - Your energy flows in a figure of eight.

The whole raison d'être for this sharing is to help us all to regain flow. To create optimal vibration that is homeostatic. Homeostatic contagion is highly beneficial for the planet and humanity.

Musical notes, color, physical vibrations, and frequencies all bring about responses in us. People may respond better to one more than the other. We have individual choices when it comes to the type of music that resonates with us. Be it classical, jazz, rock, or folk. We all know which we prefer. Colors, which of course are also vibration, influence us. We all have favorite colors. The colors we love and those we hate. Living in a room painted a color we dislike is not supportive of good health and well-being.

Being Part of the Flow

This concept has been understood within Buddhism. Buddhism teaches 'be in the flow of the water rather than being a stone on the riverbed impeding flow.' There is a wonderful Buddhist parable of a butcher who never had to sharpen his knife. He ensured that he cut only where the spaces were, never where the tough sections were, so that he never hit anything that blunted his knife.

Both in the individual and also within the collective, the key to health and well-being is to raise vibration. Humanity's successful evolution, indeed its very survival, will rely on a mass raising of vibration. Joy needs to be spread through the planet. Indeed, joy, as a high vibration, forms a key factor in the healing of the planet.

Together, compassion and love, are a lower vibration than joy. Smiles or tears are contagious.

Symbiotic relationships are necessary for successful community. Everything in nature is part of a system. Think about the animal kingdom of the Savannah of Africa. If the large predators were removed, the animals that form their prey would become too numerous, which would throw the system out of balance.

In humans there are two types of energy. Light and dark. The light represents the high vibration, the dark the low.

It is not necessary to remove all the darkness. What is required is that we embrace the darkness with light. When a room is in darkness, you switch on the light, or light a candle, hey presto, darkness suddenly disappears.

Make a habit of embracing the darkness by joining and becoming the flow.

Opening Outward

Opening outward involves expressing compassion. True, genuine, sharing. Humans can easily default to a 'primate like nature' by fighting everything they perceive as different. Compassion or sharing neutralizes this unfortunate tendency.

Connection

Energy flows in an organized fashion through the body via channels, or canals, which are made of a non-material etheric substance that the ancient Kahuna Healers of Hawaii called Aka, which means: Shadow, or, of Spiritual Essence. The Chinese call these channels Meridians and the energy chi. The Hindu's call them Nadis and the energy Prana. The Hawaiians call the energy Mana. There are many different types of channels.

The substance comprising the channels is sticky. Therefore, it attaches, then stays connected, to whatever we touch, whether that be a person or an object. The more contact we have the stronger and larger the connections become.

ENERGY FOLLOWS THOUGHT.
THOUGHTS ARE ENERGETIC HIGHWAYS.

Review

- There is only energy
- Energy has vibration, resonance and frequency
- Energy must flow to support health
- All matter is spirit first
- We are electrical beings
- Joy is a higher vibration than compassion and love combined

The Three Minds

The mind can be subdivided into three aspects (or selves):

A) Conscious

B) Unconscious

C) Superconscious or Higher Conscious Mind or Higher Self

Each of these aspects operate under prime directives specific to that aspect.

The basic teaching of the 'three selves' or 'three minds' comes from the ancient teaching of Huna from the Hawaiian Islands. The 'Kahuna' were the teachers, the healers, who promoted this concept. They knew about the three minds thousands of years ago.

The three minds (selves) were originally unified as one. Due to the 'fall' of man the minds became separated.[9] This separation causes hampered communication. We can aspire towards better communication. Developing higher levels of consciousness through raising our light quotient, together with an understanding of how the 'separated minds' function is necessary. This is why I am sharing this section with you.

In 1998 I travelled to Hawaii to study the teachings of Huna with Tad James. My understanding of the three selves or minds, stems from these teachings. Tad James MS., PhD, has played a significant role in disseminating these ancient teachings. Therefore, most of the following detail is based upon his work. This is shared with grateful thanks.

According to Tad, "the teachings of ancient Hawaii, said that as there was a Conscious Mind, there was also an Unconscious Mind. Just as there was a Conscious Mind and an Unconscious Mind, there was also a Super Conscious/Higher Conscious Mind. Each of these minds were separate, distinct from the other. Your Conscious Mind had hidden from its consciousness an Unconscious Mind, which had certain functions which were separate, distinct from the Conscious Mind.

Furthermore, there is another aspect which is also hidden from the Conscious Mind. A Higher Conscious Mind exists which also has very specific functions. This higher mind is also separate, distinct from, the Conscious Mind. What is fascinating is that the Conscious Mind cannot perceive either of these minds directly, except in certain states of consciousness."

The Conscious Mind

The Conscious mind is our free will. The manager who decides what the other two aspects of mind need to do. The initiator of decisions. Our logical, reasonable, rational aspect. The aspect we know and refer to as 'I' as in I think, I have. The Kahunas called the conscious mind

'Uhane' meaning Soul, a spirit.

According to Tad James "in the 'infinite wisdom' of the missionaries who arrived in Hawaii in 1819, it was decided that the Hawaiians were 'heathens,' that they couldn't have thought as deeply, or as logically as the newcomers from Boston. That is unfortunate, because the missionaries did not realize mental illness was virtually unknown before the arrival of the white man. Mental illness was rare because the Hawaiian Kahuna had a more highly developed system of psychology and mental health than is present even today."

In 1970, Milton Erickson,[10] M.D., had almost brought the Western perception of Psychology to the level of understanding of the ancient Hawaiians. He virtually had a complete understanding of the Conscious Mind, the Unconscious Mind, and their functions.

The Unconscious Mind

What we call the Unconscious Mind, the ancient Kahuna called 'Unihipili.' The translation of Unihipili, when taken as a whole, means Grasshopper. Have you ever heard the phrase 'grasshopper mind?' It seems to me to be a good description of how the mind flits from one thought to the next.

If we look at the meaning of the root words that make up the word Unihipili we gain even more insight into how the mind functions:

u:	The seat of our emotions from which comes feeling or grief; to stem from the heart
ni:	To pour out a liquid
hi:	To blow out with force any liquid from the mouth
pili:	To cling, stick, adhere, touch

Basically the unconscious mind was seen by the ancient Kahuna as grasshopper-like in nature, being the seat of our emotions, from which both negative and heartfelt positive feelings literally pour out, forcefully through our mouths, then cling to ourselves or others. In my opinion, a perfect description.

The Unconscious Mind is a very important part of us. Think about it for just a moment. Here's a part of us that runs our body; it makes our heart beat, causes the lymph system to circulate, our breathing to continue, our eyes to blink, our stomach to digest food, wounds to heal, plus many other tasks that we've never given a thought to.

How well do you know your Unconscious Mind? Do you consider your Unconscious Mind as a close, trusted friend? Or are you at odds with your unconscious? The ancient ones taught that really trusting and getting to know your Unconscious Mind was a very important task, indeed a first step.

The Prime Directives[11] of the Unconscious Mind

1. To store memories. Both *Temporal* which means relating to time, and *Atemporal*, which means not related to time. An example of atemporal memory would be 'How did you know you were you when you woke up this morning?' In 1960 Karl H. Pribram won the Nobel Prize for his theories of how memories are stored holographically throughout the body, not just in the brain. The Unconscious Mind is a store house for all of our memories. It is the unconscious mind that is responsible for the management of this storage, as well as the access to these memories

2. To be the domain of the emotions

3. To organize all memories

4. To repress memories with un-resolved negative emotion

5. To present repressed memories for rationalization (in order to release emotion) You've no doubt heard the saying "Everything happens for a reason." When resolution is gained, or a lesson is learned, on an emotionally charged past event the emotion disappears

6. To keep repressed emotions repressed, for protection, until choice demands otherwise

7. To run the physical body's systems such as blinking, breathing,

metabolism, healing cuts or wounds, growing hair & nails

8. To preserve the body in instinctive ways through fight or flight, or survival mechanisms, and will create strategies in childhood or under stressful conditions that are intended to aid self preservation

9. To control and maintain perceptions. Regular ones, through the five senses and telepathic ones through the energetic precedence.

10. To generate, store and transmit energy

11. To Respond with instinct or habit. In other words, it creates habitual behaviors in order to make life easier. Once you learn a skill it becomes automatic, often through 'Muscle Memory.' For example, a great golf swing. Or habitual. An anxious child-like habit of biting the nails triggers the unconscious mind to make a neurological connection between the feeling of anxiety and the action of biting nails. Every time afterwards, when anxiety is experienced, automatically the fingers go to the mouth

12. It's programmed to continually seek more, then even more. We are meant to be learning machines therefore ADD Attention Deficit Disorder cannot exist. All that is happening in the case of ADD is that someone is putting their attention on something other than what another person deems suitable at the time

13. Its language is symbolic (uses or responds to symbols). Often dreams are symbolic rather than literal and when interpreted often have significant meaning. The national flag, may, as a symbol trigger certain emotional or behavioral reactions. Symbols have often been used in religion or mythology because of the unconscious reaction they can elicit. Carl Jung[12] was the first to recognize this. He said that the Unconscious Mind creates, uses, and responds to symbols

14. It takes everything personally. This is the basis of 'Perception is Projection.' What you see in your reality is who you are. The good news is, what you say you like about your friend, is also what you like about yourself. The bad news is, that when you say what you dislike about your friend, you are also referring to

what you dislike about yourself. It's a really good idea to think the best about everybody you meet in your world. If you are a Coach or Therapist, a Teacher or a Manager for example, think the best about your clients or students. View them as being magnificent, able, willing to change. It was George Estabrooks (1943) and also Andre Weitzenhoffer (1957) who both said that what the therapist doesn't believe to be true will not be actualized by the client. Be careful because you can limit your children, clients or students with your own limiting beliefs

15. It works on principle of least effort. Takes the path of least resistance

16. To be a servant. To follow orders. It likes to be asked to help you. This can be done consciously or unconsciously. It will listen in to your moment to moment thoughts sifting through until it finds a thought it assumes is an instruction. Usually this is a thought you think most often. Be careful what you think about!

17. Is the realm of the imagination

18. It does not process a negative instruction

If you take sixteen, seventeen and eighteen I can give you a great example of how they work in unison. Don't think about a large pink elephant standing next to you. Don't think about that big pink elephant. What happens? In your imagination a wonderful large elephant appears right next to you. Wait a minute, I said do not think about the elephant. You however, did think about the elephant. What went wrong? Well, the unconscious mind cannot process a negated instruction. It ignores the word NOT. Rolls right over it as if it's invisible. When we say to ourselves numerous times a day 'I don't want to feel anxious' guess what message the servant, whose job it is to create anxiety, receives. Of course. I want to feel anxious. If you monitor your moment to moment thoughts, you will be amazed what you are programming yourself to do! As soon as you become aware of an erroneous instruction immediately say to yourself, Stop! Cancel! Cancel! It will have the effect of pressing the delete key. Then you can immediately say 'it' the way you want it. For example, 'I want to feel calm.'

Many branches of western psychology view the Unconscious Mind as an adversary or an uncivilized child that needs dominating or training.

In contrast the ancient wisdom reminds us to respect the unconscious. To appreciate its contribution to our health and well-being.

The Superconscious Mind or Higher Self

The great Kahuna, Daddy Bray, who lived in Kona, Hawaii until his death in 1968, said that "mankind is made up of both material and spiritual parts," in other words made up equally of matter and spirit. Should that be the case, then the wholeness of our Being has not yet been recognized by traditional western psychology.

The Kahuna say that we are also a Higher Conscious Mind. The term used in ancient times was '**Aumakua,**' meaning:

Au:	spirit; your spirit or mine, or the spirit of another person.
Makua:	Parent, older, senior, mature; or to sustain.

If we add these meanings together, we create the first prime directive of the Higher Self: to be a totally trustworthy guardian and parental spirit. There are fifteen others.

Prime Directives of the Super Conscious Mind or Higher Self

- To be a totally trustworthy guardian and parental spirit
- Is the Divine Spirit in the individual
- Connection with Higher Self makes everything alright
- Totally balanced male and female energy
- An expression of Man and Woman's own innate perfection
- Our connection to the Higher Realms of creation
- Takes control of our personal evolution

- Has the power to recognize both root causes or origins
- Has the power to remove fixations, complexes and identifications, and conduct healing on demand
- Has the power to attain extra sensory perception (ESP) and develop intuition
- Has the power to know, predict probable outcomes and affect the future
- Never makes mistakes
- Cannot interfere with the Conscious Mind's free will (must await invite)
- Is all forgiving because we are all connected. As such we are all one
- The Conscious Mind has the free will to deny Prime Directives of the Higher Self (and just might do it if the Ego is strong enough)
- It's the aspect whose natural domain is the 'higher heart space' or the 'Space of Pure Potential'[13]

Next, what is the relationship between the three minds of mankind, and how are they connected?

As you look at figure 4, notice the connections:

There is a connection between the Conscious Mind and the Unconscious Mind. Indeed, the flow of energy and information goes both ways.

There is also a connection between the Unconscious Mind and the Higher Conscious Mind. Information and energy flows both ways.

There is no direct connection however between the Conscious Mind and the Higher Conscious Mind.

Even so, the Higher Conscious Mind may communicate with us by way of energy and information enveloping us, by "falling down" from above.

An ancient chant says:

"Li ta I'o o ka'auhelemoa la"
"I tremble; I have goose flesh;

the I'o comes inside me because
of the continuously falling fine rain."

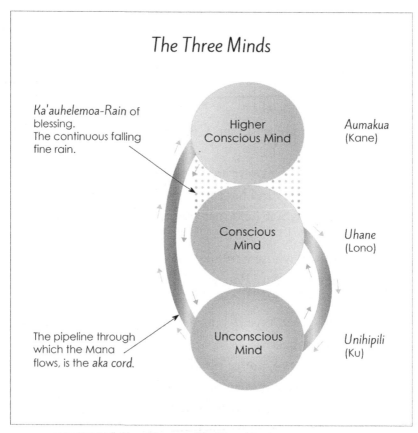

Figure 4 – The Three Minds.

The **Ka'auhelemoa** is well known in Hawaii. It's a fine rain with tiny drops that blows off the mountains. When it reaches you, you feel it, yet when you touch your skin, it's dry.

Connectedness: Each of the minds is connected to the other by means of life force energy, called, in the Hawaiian system, **Mana**. Also known as Chi in China. Ki in Japan. Prana in Indian Sanskrit. Spiritus in Latin. Ruach in Hebrew. Orgone energy according to Wilhelm Reich.[14] Wakan by the North American Lakota People. Wong[15] among the Ghanaians of the Gold Coast.

Some of these words means Breath. Every one of them means Life.

Review
- There are three aspects to the human mind due to the 'Fall'
- The conscious, unconscious, and super/higher conscious
- Energy carries information flow between them
- For reasons of health it's a good idea to build rapport with, to improve communication with, the unconscious mind, as it controls the body
- Emotions, energy, and imagination are under the auspices of the unconscious mind
- There is no communication between the conscious mind and the higher conscious mind except that which 'rains down' via the intuition
- There is direct communication between the conscious and the unconscious minds. And also between the unconscious and higher conscious

Specific, Correct Questioning Gets Results

When I was training in NLP I learned about the so called 'Meta Model.' A specific questioning technique that is invaluable when wishing to gain insights or get to the root of a problem. It was modelled on the work of Virginia Satir, who was widely regarded as the 'Mother of Family Therapy.' Satir's results in her counselling practice were based on unpacking and getting into the details of people's issues.

The Meta Model is based on four questions that solve problems by deliberately getting into the sometimes minute, details: -

How?

What?

When?

Who?

Did you notice that *'why'* was omitted? Does that surprise you?

'Why' is perhaps the most common question we ask, yet in the context of healing it is the absolute worst question we can ask. 'Why' engages the ego. Why triggers defensiveness. It gives the conscious mind something to latch onto. It never gets into the detail in a way that is useful. How? What? When? or Who? elicit useful information. These questions are always answered by the unconscious mind in a helpful way.

Ask questions such as:

- What is the purpose of the discomfort I'm feeling?
- When did this emotion I'm feeling really originate?
- How did the issue _____X_____ start?
- Does this __X___ serve any positive purpose at this time?
- How do I do this self-defeating strategy of _____X_____?
- What does this pattern _____X___ have to teach me?
- Is this triggered by a particular person or experience?
- Is this issue my cross to bear?
- Will I ever be ready for change?
- Is this a major life lesson that I must learn fully and completely?

Any other expanding, open ended questions, that do not limit the answer by the nature of the question, are useful. For example: -
What's next? Or, *What if?* Both these questions lead to forward movement.

During an emotional storm ask, 'How is this helping?' This takes the awareness outside the storm. It helps you see the bigger picture.

When Is Asking 'Why' Useful?

Why? Is useful in two contexts only. One is when discovering your deeply held values. As in, why is trust important to me? Or why is co-operation from others important to me in relationships? The other is when you are goal setting. You write down all the reasons 'why' you want to achieve a particular goal. Asking 'why' in this context helps you feel the driving emotion behind the goal. It helps you get clearly focused. When you get the why's behind what you want then you start to vibrate at that rate which in turn helps you magnetize what you want. If you imagine being successful, you will begin to vibrate to success. Then you will attract success together with the opportunities you need.

When you verbalize your goal, together with why you want it, your energy changes. You get into your 'Center.' Then you vibrate in alignment with your 'Core.' This is important. When you vibrate in harmony with your core, you are connected to your Higher Self. Your Higher Self may then assist you to magnetize the situations, synchronicities, or opportunities your actions will create.

In NLP we use a technique called 'dissociation' where you visualize yourself having achieved your goal. (Goal setting is discussed in Chapter Five in more detail). You see yourself in the future having attained what you want. This is different to being associated looking out of your own eyes in the moment of now. As you start to see yourself in a future scenario (dissociated) you will begin to vibrate as if you are in the future. That future point then links to the now point, hence you vibrate in the now in harmony with the future point. In other words, you are vibrating as if you have already achieved the goal.

Not

Remember the unconscious mind cannot process the word 'Not' therefore self-talk should always be positively stated rather than using a negation.

If you don't believe me try another experiment: Don't think about a large red rabbit. What do you see in your mind's eye? Because the process of imagination is a function of the unconscious mind and because the unconscious mind cannot, not, give us what we ask for, then we get what we asked for, just as if the word 'Not' was omitted from the instruction.

For example, rather than say 'I don't want to worry' say 'I trust the process of life.' Remember if you do make the error of thinking or saying a negatively phrased instruction immediately say 'Stop, cancel, cancel.' This has the effect of pressing the delete button. Then you can replace what you have deleted with the positive opposite.

Instead of saying "I will not be processing for other people." Better would be, "I choose to process only my own stuff. Everyone else's toxic thought trash and low vibrational energy is either transmuted safely now by the violet flame or returned from whence it came, for the benefit of all."

Imagination and Creativity

Let's talk about creativity.

If we create our own reality, how do we do it?

Answer: Imagination.

Ancient Hermetic philosophy, the early Tibetan schools, together with certain Western alchemists, all agreed on that answer. Imagination is what makes us powerful. Imagination is a function of the unconscious mind.

The unconscious mind cannot discern what we imagine from what we see 'out there', from what we call 'reality' perceived through our third dimensional senses. This being the case we can choose to imagine the reality we want to experience consciously.

> To be or not to be, that is the question.
> Well, not exactly.
> To attach one's self to another's reality or invent one's own reality, that is the question.
>
> -JON RAPPOPORT

Or we can fall into the trap of unconsciously imagining a reality we would rather avoid, then have to live in it ignorant of the fact that we have created our own suffering.

If there is a problem, you have your imagination as a tool to create the solution. You are the one who holds the power to solve a problem or make it even bigger.

Jon Rappoport[16] puts it this way. "You are the dynamic force. You are the initiator. You are the one who asks a question then answers it. You are the one who surmounts the notion of problems and, by inventing reality, gets out ahead of chronic problems. I'm selling you to you." He goes on to say that most people, if they have any interest beyond the details of daily life, are looking for a metaphysical structure "they can they hang their hats on." They hope they can find a metaphysic 'out there' that explains life, and existence, then, by attaching their thoughts to it they will find greater illumination and consciousness." Jon maintains, "this solution brings diminishing returns over time. Why? Because what they are seeking is obscuring an unavoidable fact: they themselves are the answer. Beyond any existence. The individual is his own answer. His answer rests in what he decides to create."

Jon continues with "a person can tap dance around this central fact or ignore it. He can ignore it for a year, a decade, a century, a thousand or a million incarnations, wherever and however he incarnates or exists, in whatever spaces or places or realms... but he will keep coming back to it.

To be or not to be, that is the question. Well, not exactly. To attach one's self to another's reality or invent one's own reality, that is the question. No one, except for the person who is asking, can deliver the answer. Then act on it."

Brain Function

Gamma, Beta, Alpha, Theta, and Delta are different levels of consciousness, of brain activity. Each one is ideally suited for different outcomes.

Brainwaves

Electrical activity in the form of nerve impulses is happening within the brain at all times, even during sleep. Cessation of this activity only happens at so called 'brain death.' The amount of activity varies from moment to moment. This activity can be measured using a device known as an EEG electrode. The composite nerve impulse activity recorded is called an electroencephalogram or EEG.

Wherever an EEG electrode is placed on the scalp it will mainly detect the activity in that brain region. However, it should be noted that the electrodes receive the electrical impulses from thousands of neurons. In fact, one square millimeter of cortex has more than 100,000 neurons. It is only when the input to a region is synchronized with electrical activity occurring at the same time, that you begin to distinguish simple periodic waveforms in the EEG.

Five simple periodic rhythms recorded in the EEG are gamma, beta, alpha, theta and delta. These rhythms are identified by frequency (Hz or cycles/sec) and amplitude. The amplitudes recorded by scalp electrodes are in the range of microvolts (μV or 1/1,000,000 of a volt).

Rhythm	State	Frequency (Hz)	Amp (μV)
gamma	Highly functional, Extra Sensory perception. Fast neuron activity.	30-45	10-100
beta	Fully awake. Normal thinking, conscious, state.	13-30	5-10
alpha	Relaxed. Heightened sense of well-being. The body consciousness begins to listen to the conscious mind.	8-13	20-200
theta	Dreamy. Achieved when visualizing in meditative state.	4-8	10
delta	Deep sleep or deeply meditative state achieved by experienced meditators.	1-5	20-200

According to Bruce Lipton our brain waves in the first two years of life are the equivalent of delta with occasional theta as measured by EEG. This creates the most programmable state in the child thus activating and forming what we call the unconscious mind.

After the age of six the brain begins to operate at higher levels. It goes into alpha for the first time. This correlates with the appearance of the conscious mind at around seven years old. Until age six the brain is programmed to rapidly download the beliefs and the behaviors it observes in others, into memory.

At around twelve years of age the brain can achieve the beta level of consciousness which is sustained high level electrical activity. This explains how the agendas of the conscious, and unconscious minds, are generally very different. The unconscious mind is often called the shadow self because it operates as programmed without conscious intervention. The unconscious mind is like a juke box playing unconsciously chosen behaviors. There is no point yelling at the jukebox to stop, you have to take physical action and press a button to make another choice. This action is will power. However, how much easier would life have been if the conditioning had been resourceful in the first place? Garnering will power later is often challenging. Once conceived, the fetus tunes into the father's and mother's every thought, every action. It also receives information from the external environment surrounding the mother, even though it is in the womb. Conscious parenting is a valuable foundation for health and well-being.

The Purest Way to Health Is by Gently Taming, Kindly Calming, the Mind

When in the **Alpha** state there is a sense of peaceful residing. Of well-being. There is no attachment to outcome. No conflict or fight occurring. There is less ability to speak in the normal way. However, speech is possible. It may just be slower, quieter, and with fewer words used. Resistance is possible in this state. Many athletes utilize this state in order to focus on their outcome. The term 'being in the zone' has been coined to describe this easily accessible resourceful state.

Theta state is a conscious, deeply meditative yet active state, often associated with visualization or dreams. If one tried to stand when in this state, there would be a 'woozy feeling.' Speech is difficult. The person is highly suggestible and will respond without resistance. Truths can be discovered in this state. During deep healing, when the brain is in re-set mode, we naturally achieve this state. If you used to believe healing was hard work, then you can change that right now to 'healing is easy, effortless.' Whatever you choose when in this state, you can create. Healing does not need to be hard work. It's effortless, and easy. Whatever you choose to create you can create. I have recorded meditations to enable you to access this state of consciousness for both healing and evolutionary purposes.

Gamma – heightened brain function and extra sensory perception is possible. There is extremely fast neurological activity.

Delta – deep sleep or the deeply meditative state of a very experienced meditator. Sometimes achieved when deliberately sending compassionate thoughts of healing remotely to another person.

Beta – normal awake state

The energy of the heartbeat is stronger than the energy of brain waves. Hence, I use the energy of the heart for healing purposes.

Review

- Learn to ask the right questions to get results
- Avoid 'Not'
- Use your imagination
- Learn to tame your mind

CHAPTER 2
FINDING THE SCIENCE, THE SACRED GEOMETRY

My brain is only a receiver.
In the Universe there is a core from which we obtain
knowledge, strength and inspiration.
— NIKOLA TESLA

THE **ORGANIC LAWS** of Multi-dimensional Physics are the genuine sacred science. A great deal of what we have been taught in Science Class is erroneous and I hope to pique your curiosity, and encourage you to become more discerning about what you read or hear, by sharing a little of my knowledge derived from both in depth research and spirit guidance.

The Quantum and the Newtonian (mechanical) world view together, create conflict in people's minds. This causes imbalance. This is why I felt this section was crucial. I will endeavor to simply explain the truth of how our reality is created and how it functions.

The Torus

What is the torus? Torus (plural tori) are shapes, patterns of energy, formed as a result of waves of electricity.

What a torus looks like and how it interacts with vortices and other aspects of sacred geometry is the subject of argument.

Nassim Haramein, Marco Rodin, the movie *Thrive*, together with many others, depict the tube torus with external vortices as in figure 5. They speak of the white hole as an emitter and the black hole as an absorber. The zero point as a tiny space of no-thing in between the two vortices. This form of Torus has been termed the Toroidal Vortex Model.

My Guides described an aspect of the structure containing the Torus as a plane stretching into infinity with two nipples, one on the top and one underneath. This caused me to question the commonly depicted Toroidal Vortex Model (Figure 5). I began to seek what I came to call the 'Plane Torus' and was delighted to find it.

As with all energetic unseen constructs we may only become acquainted with the real nature of the construct if we accurately perceive it psychically.

Dr. Walter Russell[1] saw metaphysical structures psychically with his acute clairvoyance. In May of 1921 he had an out-of-body experience he called *Cosmic Illumination*. New knowledge was revealed to him 'in the Light' as he put it. Debates with scientists and several books followed as he tried to explain his new knowledge.

His version of the structure of the torus complete with the male and female electrical vortices, and zero point *sphere*, releasing energy out into a plane, is known as 'The Spiral Vortex Model' in Russellian Science (Figure 5). Dr. Russell said that the vortices were male and female electrical generators both spinning in the same direction. The three tori within the vortices were tonal resonators.

The Organic Laws of Multi-dimensional Physics is the genuine sacred science and I believe the Russellian interpretation is the most correct. It is closer to the Council of Truth's description.

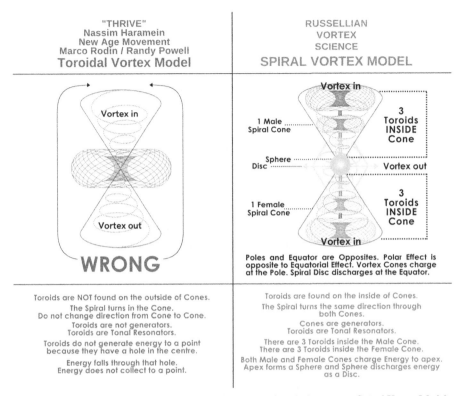

Figure 5 – The erroneous Toroidal Vortex Model compared with the accurate Spiral Vortex Model.

Let us look at another vortex type structure, the chakra. I feel the chakra structure, as we have come to know it, supports the Russellian Science 'Spiral Vortex Model.'

Chakras as Vortices

We know that chakras are spinning vortices of energy. We know there is a back and a front vortex, both taking energy into the chakra. We can feel it with our hands when we scan the energy field. We know that when the energy gets into the body it spreads through the energy system and through the nervous system. It moves up and down the spine and beyond.

The Tube Torus

The Tube Torus is similar to a donut in shape. Torus comes from the latin word for cushion.

Electrical engineers are very familiar with Tube Tori. Typically a copper torus transformer may have an input of 220V with an output of 110V. In other words a torus is a transformer. In a chakra the energy may be transformed to become more refined by the tori in the vortices before it enters the body.

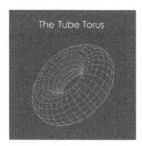

Figure 6 - The Tube Torus.

Ascension Mechanics

Ascension mechanics tells us that in order to ascend we need to awaken our Higher Heart Chakra. My Guidance told me, and together with many clients and students I have confirmed by direct experience, that the Higher Heart gives us access to a place ouptside of our space time continuum that is often perceived as an enormous spherical space. I believe we are experiencing the zero point sphere.

I call the Higher Heart Chakra the Space of Pure Potential (SPP) because when we reside there we are no longer bound by the constraints of our third dimensional human-ness. We are unlimited and have easier access to our higher dimensional selves such as our Soul and Monad. We also find it easier to connect with all other people, together with non-physical beings dwelling in other dimensions.

We may access the zero point sphere, within the center of the Higher Heart's male and female vortices, to both transform and transmute our issues and un-create them.

Electricity as Creator

In Russellian science electricity is not termed positive and negative. It is termed male and female. Polarity and sex are one. The only cause of vibration is polarity. Both male and female are different aspects of positive. There is no negative. A dual electric Universe seeks stability via the pairing of opposites that create a rhythmic balanced interchange. Twin opposing electrical vortices that seek equilibrium by coming together. When they come together they rest in the still center. The stillness could be termed magnetic. Magnetism is an aspect of electricity not a separate force.

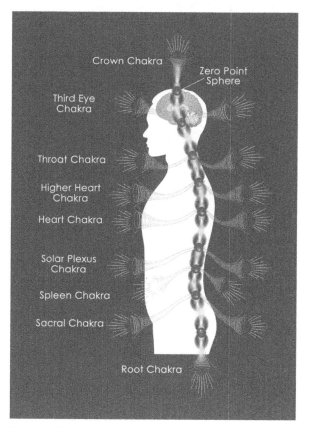

Figure 7 - Chakras each have a zero point sphere located between the two electrical vortices.

If you wish to explore this further I suggest researching the work of Dr. Walter Russell, Dewey B Larson, Robert Otey,[2] and Ashayana Deane (Keylonta Science).

This male and female electricity constantly being drawn to come together to seek equilibrium and stillness could be thought of as the macrocosm.

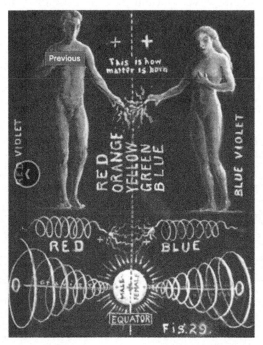

Figure 8 – Dr. Walter Russell's diagram of how matter is born. The male and female electrical vortices seek each other out and when they connect the movement becomes stillness. Then the still sphere emits energy out of the plane (here termed equator).

The microcosm would be the loving sexual union of a man and woman following the experience of a 'magnetic' attraction to each other.

If you look at figure 8 which shows how matter is born you will notice colors are mentioned. Red, Orange on the male side, Green and Blue on the female side and yellow in the center. Many years ago I heard that in ancient times girls were dressed in blue and boys in red/pink. I found this interesting given that today it's the opposite. Girls/pink. Boys/blue. I remember yellow romper suits were knitted during the 50's and 60's if the sex of the child was unknown prior to birth. Perhaps clothes color choice depends on whether there is a desire to balance the sexes or enhance them.

Light

You are familiar with the term 'Light' (with a capital L) in the context of healing. Light, and light, are electrical waves. Space is filled with 'Light.' The sun shines its light which we may 'see' with our eyes because light is in fact rapidly pulsing spiraling electric wave forms. Space is *omnipresent stillness*. All that exists is different pressure conditions of electricity, otherwise known as 'Light.' Light travels in spirals at different rates. Omnipresent stillness is present in the zero point sphere. The vortices are moving. Stillness is the cause of motion. Light moves in spiraling waves. Light has no particles (photons are a misnomer) because its form is electrical wave. Electricity is the full working force of the Universe.

Figure 9 - Tornados are a visual example of the 'spiral vortex model' in action. The eye of the storm is an example of the zero point sphere and the stillness in the shaft.

Walter Russell stated in his book *The Secret of Light* "The un-created universe is Light Undivided. The Created Universe is Light divided into mated pairs."

Tornadoes as Electrically Generated Vortices

Tornedos are a visual example of the 'spiral vortex model' in action. The eye of the storm is an example of the zero point sphere and the stillness in the shaft.

Now might be the time to mention that the North and South Poles of the Earth both charge inwards towards each other, and a zero point sphere is created at the core of the earth.

While we are speaking of earth phenomena think about Lightning. A tremendous natural high voltage electrical discharge which surely demonstrates that electricity is naturally present everywhere.

Figure 10 - The Spiral Vortex Model showing stillness in the center and spiral movement at the outside. Here both vortices draw in energy. The upper is male and the lower is female. They seek union, or equilibrium. They meet in the center. The central zero point sphere is omnipresent stillness full of pure potential.

The Plane Torus or Spiral Vortex Model

I need to make it clear that only the 'Spiral Vortex' (Figure 10), is utilized in my healing methodology to un-create issues. It's an open system. The other erroneous 'Toroidal vortex model' is a closed system and as such cannot transform and transmute distorted energy into its original state of pure unadulterated Light. I will explain more about my methodology in due course.

Gyroscope

A gyroscope is a device that contains a disc turning on an axis (Figure 11). When the disc is spinning the device stabilizes and stands upright of its own accord. When the disc is still the structure cannot remain upright it must rest on a supporting surface. Gyroscopes maintain a stable orientation in space by the nature of their spin. We have our own energetic gyroscope. We will cover this more in the hara lines section because Hara Lines one and two form the axis of the gyroscope. However, I wanted to point out that the gyroscope reminds me of the nature of the Spiral Vortex model.

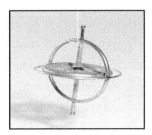

Figure 11 - A gyroscope is a device that contains a disc turning on an axis.

Humans as Electrical Beings

It always fascinates me that people, medical personnel included, have difficulty accepting that we are electrical in nature.

An electrocardiogram (EKG or ECG) is a test that checks for problems with the electrical activity of the heart.

An ECG shows the heart's electrical activity as line tracings on paper. The spikes, the dips in the tracings, are called waves. This medical test proves the electrical nature of the heart. Of our whole being.

> The electric energy which motivates us is not within our bodies at all. It is a part of the universal supply which flows through us from the Universal Source with an intensity set by our desires and our will.
>
> – DR. WALTER RUSSELL

In humans the energy flows in, both through the crown of the head and through the feet. It is bi-directional. In other words, it flows like the tides, one way then the next. In the matrix of this flow are the electrical waves that structure or govern the nurturing 'cosmic' energy from which we are crystallized.

I hope you will now agree that I have made a good enough case to support the Russellian Science model of the nature of creation, and the electrical energy of creation.

Universal Physics and Unified Field Theory

Let's explore a very short introduction to the Unified Field Theory. Unified Physics shows the holistic nature of the universe. Two thousand four hundred years ago Plato said that the Universe is a single creature. After nearly fourteen billion years of evolution on Earth we now have the science to change the traditional world view that everything is separate. The science to prove we are Cosmic Beings.

> Although the truth is easily stated as "All Is One" the sages have said that the realization of this truth in the core of one's being can take many lifetimes"
>
> - RAVI RAVINDRA, SCIENCE AND THE SACRED

Many great thinkers and physicists have postulated that space is not empty. In fact, space is full of electrical energy as we have discussed. John A Wheeler, a collaborator of Einstein, said. "No point is more central than this: empty space is not empty. It is the seat of the most violent physics."

Everything emerges from this not-empty vacuum but dense full of energy space. Vacuum energy produces our reality. I prefer the term *omnipresent stillness*, to vacuum. David Bohm said, "Space is not empty. It is full…. The Universe is not separate from this cosmic sea of energy."

The presence of energy in the stillness was ignored for over one hundred years because it was intimidating to the modern physics community.

Space defines our material world. Not the other way round. Space is a substance template for matter. Matter is indeed 'spirit first' because space is teeming with invisible 'spirit,' invisible electrical energy, invisible 'life-force.'

Spiritual Science was the only science until it became opposed by Natural Science.

Natural Science ignores the existence of spirit in matter. It is a mechanistic Newtonian view.

The Zero Point Sphere

The zero point sphere contains infinite 'mass' but appears to be an empty space.

The zero point is actually a 'not empty' space as already discussed. This full space is teeming with possibilities. This full space connects all things. It is the similarity in all things. The sameness that connects. It is the omnipresent stillness from which movement is birthed.

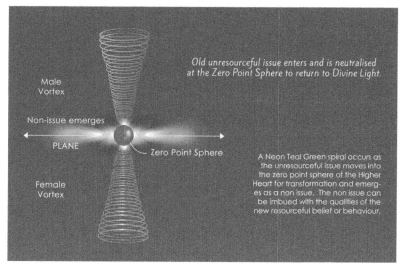

Figure 12 - The zero point sphere first neutralizes, then recycles old issues.

The zero point sphere is a recycling plant. Whatever distortion goes in is transformed. Vortices, both male and female, absorb and direct energy, with information attached, to the zero point, for transformation into pure undistorted potential energy once again. Whatever information the electrical energy waves were holding is released because it is un-created. Because energy never dies it just changes form, the recycled energy thus created can be re-used. Intention stemming from the consciousness of a sentient being, then directs this recycled, now pure potential energy, to become 'some-thing.' The observer affects the observed. This is true for all dimensions, all universes, because it happens in the smallest and the largest. As above, so below. Fractally. More about this concept later.

We as humans can use the zero point to un-create an issue and create a resource.

The Zero Point Sphere Recycles Our Issues

During a healing session with me, my friend Tanya observed, with psychic sight, the change in the energy of an issue she wanted to release. She saw a green spiral as the old issue was inverting through the zero point sphere. On emergence into the plane the energy was 'non-issue' with very pale yellowish color.

The green light is perceived when the pattern of the issue is moving through the central portion of the female vortex.

The new thing is a no-thing. The new no-thing can then be imbued with the new pattern of preferred reaction or behavior. For example, releasing the limiting belief of 'I'm not worthy' firstly neutralizes then secondly becomes the preferred belief of 'I am worthy.'

The Space of Pure Potential

Let's remember that all matter is spirit, energy, first and foremost. Individual perception assists in proving this fact. Each person perceives in a unique way. For example, the color-blind person perceives color differently. The saying 'beauty is in the eyes of the beholder' speaks volumes. There is no hard or fast truth, only individual perception.

Spirituality

All cultures have their own terms to acknowledge Life Force Energy. Chi in China, Ki in Japan, Prana in India, Mana in Hawaii, Wakan in Native American tradition, being just a few. The Holy Spirit is the Christian term for the life force energy that is present before physical matter can form. Recall the first words of the Bible – "In the beginning was the Word." In other words, vibration was present first (in the beginning). The Bible refers to the so called 'Holy Spirit' being present before matter was created.

We are eternal beings in a temporary physical form.

Potential

In an effort to explain potential, in this context of all matter is spirit first, let's take a look at waves as they wash up on the beach. The waves move the sand. First pushing it in one direction as the tide moves in, then pulling it in the opposite direction, as the wave moves out. Ripples are created in the sand as a result of the tidal flow.

Consider potential. It interacts with human beings in the following way:

- Sand is the potential (non-resistant, malleable)
- Waves are the movement of energy
- The Pattern in the sand is the human being

In the zero point, there is a moment of suspension, as it were. In that moment we are able to be influenced. Just as the sand on the beach is influenced by the waves. When waves wash up the beach, the sand is first pushed in one direction. Then the receding tide pulls in the opposite direction. In this way, all the grains of sand ebb and flow in unison, rather than separately, as lonely individual tiny pieces. Ripples are created in the sand as a result of the tidal flow. In us the sand represents our potential. The waves the movement of energy. The resulting pattern is the human being as we are at any moment in time. Of course this pattern is open to change at any time through the use of free will, or through personal choice.

Figure 13 - Ripples created in the sand as a result of tidal flow.

That is the focus of this book. It is the key. We contemplate how the sand could move differently. Methodology is just pieces, parts of that key element. Our intention in a healing session is to enable all the grains of sand to ebb and flow in unison rather than separately, as individual tiny pieces. The intention is to bring healing to enable the person to get back into balance so all becomes possible.

Our Personal Space of Pure Potential

In the Spiral Vortex Model, at the point where the vortices meet, in the Zero Point Sphere energy field, we find a special still place. This space has one purpose only. To energize and enliven living organisms. It also neutralizes harmful frequencies. It increases spiritual awareness, a sense of oneness. It is our higher consciousness.

This is ostensibly a void of still nothingness, yet it contains the pure potential energy that we can use to create or un-create whatever we wish. In fact, I have coined the term the Personal 'Space of Pure Potential' to describe the zero point sphere within the Higher Heart chakra. Learning how to harness the power of this Space of Pure Potential (SPP) is the key to tapping into our fully conscious empowered being-ness. This Zero Point Energy Field or SPP is the gate to accessing pure potential energy. It can only be entered however, by using the power of intention, also known as will. This is not personal egoic will-power, but our heart based will. Will, when accessed in Theta state, enables harnessing the potential. Some people have difficulty engaging their will therefore I will discuss this in the Hara Line chapter.

Zero Point Field

The Zero Point is the 'Moment of Suspension' in Humans.

Everyone has a 'zero point' sphere within them filled with pure potential. A tiny place yet with a vast openness. Yes, that sounds contrary to our limited third dimensional perception, yet it is true. What's more, to feel the expansion all you need to do is go there. We will learn how to do this later.

There are many zero points in our energetic make up. The one that we are the most interested in here, in the context of healing, is the Higher Heart's zero point sphere. When I refer to the Space of Pure Potential I am referring specifically to the Higher Heart's zero point sphere.

This is the place of infinite pure potential. The 'Suspension Point' as the Guides term it, is accessed here. (more about that later). Misperceptions together with other issues, such as low vibrational emotions, or limiting beliefs, can go into that zero point sphere to be recycled. They emerge changed. Big shifts can come about. Or small tiny changes. When the shifts are huge or extreme people can fall down or pass out. Just like when someone receives news that is shocking, the legs go weak. Forcing a need to sit, or lie down, because we 'go weak at the knees' through a lack of energetic flow or a re-directed energetic flow.

Reason for Being Here

Every person has chosen to be living on Earth at this time. Each person has a reason for being here. The choice to incarnate was made freely. The choice of life purpose or life lessons was made equally freely. Through the methods mentioned in this book, you will discover that you can experience what you chose to experience. You may find your way again. You are able to assist clients who are temporarily lost.

All Human Beings Are the Same, There Is No Difference

Perceived separation is the battle humanity is fighting. It's not about good or evil or various belief systems. It's not that simple. The dangerous mindset is 'they are not like us therefore we can kill them or take from them with impunity.'

The sad fact is that unless separatist behavior stops, we will exterminate ourselves as a species.

No doubt you have heard the term 'butterfly effect' which was coined by Edward Norton Lorenz.[3]

In chaos theory the butterfly effect is the sensitive dependence on initial conditions in which a small change in one state of a deterministic nonlinear system, can result in large differences in a later state. Some refer to it as the Domino effect. In other words, it's the idea, that small causes may have large effects. It is a basic Universal Law of Physics.

In the year 1800, Johann Gottlieb Fichte[4] said, "You could not remove a single grain of sand from its place without thereby changing something throughout all parts of the immeasurable whole."

What we need to realize is that each one of us has the power to change humanity. We also have the power to change the Earth through choice, whether in a small or a large way. This is because we are all connected. Each kind thought we have, reverberates through humanity. Each judgmental, critical, carping, merciless, unforgiving, uncharitable, discriminating, rejective, or fault finding thought we have, or word we speak, reverberates through humanity. Indulging in judgment is a dangerous behavior. Inferences are always based on judgment.

Judgment comes first: 'this is to this, as this is not to this.' The original judgment comes first. Charitable, undiscriminating, forgiving, uncritical, accepting behaviors or thoughts are the opposite of judgment. If every person's perception is unique how can it be appropriate to judge? Don't judge a man until you have walked a mile in his shoes, states the old adage. Judgments based on erroneous perceptions or misunderstandings reverberate through humanity. A small causal act, with a potentially enormous effect. Just like the drop of water falling into a pool of water can reverberate out to the very edge of the pool. It's crucial that we become aware of the energy we are sending out via our thoughts, deeds, or actions. We can heal or hurt the whole. It's our choice.

'As above, so below' is a concept we have already mentioned. The health of the species, together with the health of the individual, is inextricably linked. Individual health is not achieved in pieces and parts of the body. Health comes through a holistic approach. The health of humanity, the health of the Earth, cannot be achieved in full until every aspect of the wholeness is healthy.

When I first learned to meditate, a natural consequence was an ability to release patterns, negative emotions, that had ceased to serve me.

I suddenly became highly motivated to clear out the storage room of old unwanted items. I wanted to tidy drawers, re-arrange furniture. I was motivated to 'spring clean.' I thought nothing of it at the time. Then I started to teach meditation. The feedback from students began to tell of their undeniable urges to clean up, to declutter attics or cupboards. I then realized that internal change is always reflected in the outside environment. As within, so without. I wondered if the reflection would work the other way. I began advising clients to clear out the old hoarded unwanted stuff in their homes. The results were amazing. Suddenly new things started to appear in people's lives because space had been created to allow them in. This worked both externally and internally. In fact, I knew the clients who procrastinated in the clean-up homework weren't yet ready to let go of their issues. If we take the concept to the next level, a global clear up, together with respect for the environment, comes as a result of a rise in consciousness. One person at a time we can make a difference. We can save the planet.

The Higher Heart Space: The Space of Pure Potential

The Higher Heart zero point space is ubiquitous. In other words, omnipresent, ever-present, extensive, far-reaching, wide-ranging, all-pervasive, global, universal, inescapable.

The Higher Heart Space, the Space of Pure Potential (SPP), is the key to health, well-being, peace in the world, and abundance for all. It is the key to the end of the illusion of separateness, which fuels bigotry and hatred. I encourage you, if you are searching for change, to learn how to enter into the SPP. Then learn how to use the pure potential accessed as a result, to empower and heal yourself.

The Higher Heart Chakra Versus the Heart Chakra[5]

The Green Heart chakra is situated on the same horizontal plane as the physical heart. This chakra energizes our own physical heart. It plays a personal role in our lives. If we are too 'open hearted' the energy of this chakra can become depleted, especially if the people in receipt of our heart energy cannot, or will not, reciprocate. When the energy of the heart becomes depleted to a great extent then we feel 'depressed.' If it gets further depleted, then heart attacks can occur as the physical heart becomes constricted due to lack of energy.

The Higher Heart Chakra is the color dark teal.

The Higher Heart Chakra is located in between the green heart and the blue throat chakras. At the area of the Thymus gland. Dark Teal is a combination of green, blue, and yellow. Dark teal is a deeper color than turquoise.

The green of the heart combines with the blue of the throat, together with the yellow of the Solar Plexus.

The Solar Plexus energy is designed to empower us if we use it wisely. (Of course, it can disempower if we are unawakened, have limited beliefs, or are emotionally or mentally in need of healing). The Throat chakra enables us to speak our truth. Imagine a combination of self-empowerment, love, and truth. The Higher Heart gives us access to this.

The Higher Heart can play a role in service to humanity. When we are evolved enough the Higher Heart chakra activates. It then becomes the best chakra through which to relate to the world. Evolution is supported by undergoing our healing journey, releasing low vibrational emotions, achieving both emotional and mental balance, mastering the ego and raising our vibration. It has the strength to never be depleted.

Irrespective of how others treat us, we are unfazed because of the natural inherent strength we feel.

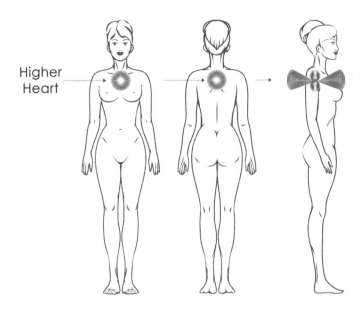

Higher
Heart

The color of the Higher Heart Chakra is dark teal.
We can create, and co-create with our Creator, on a much higher level
when we are residing in the higher heart. When in the now moment,
together with being in this space, we may heal ourselves, assist others
in their healing and alignment, and Mother Earth, without exhausting
our energy reserves.

Figure 14 – The location of the dark teal Higher Heart Chakra.

I would suggest that you consciously begin to explore your Higher Heart space. It is through this space that we can easily connect to our Soul. We also imbue all that we create with high vibrational energies. We are better placed to radiate our light out into the world.

Other people can never deplete our Higher Heart energy. It is fed by inexhaustible Source and Earth energy that firstly join in the Solar Plexus, then find their way up to the Higher Heart. Source and Earth energies can meet in the heart when we are working on ourselves in healing and meditation.

Set the intention to open and then live from your Higher Heart. Your Space of Pure Potential.

Other people will never feel threatened if you are living from your SPP when you interact with them.

I live from my open Higher Heart. My SPP. When I teach or work with people, I naturally protect my own green heart chakra by working from my Higher Heart. In that way my energy stays high. In addition, my energy, and my nervous system, remain unaffected by the energy of others. I also set the intention to empower others. My Solar Plexus energy helps with that.

Open heartedness at the green chakra level should only be an intention when relating with a person who is in love with you, or loves you. Furthermore, someone who would never act in a way that will deplete your heart.

Heart depletion behaviors in others include betrayal, narcissism, sociopathic or psychopathic behaviors, or stubborn resistance.

Broken hearts are green hearts that have been subjected to 'insults' (aka trauma), dense energies or depletion whilst very open. They can be healed. The healing process is an opportunity to awaken, in addition to opening the turquoise Higher Heart, in order to support living from there.

The color turquoise aids mass communication. Coral, the opposite of turquoise, is related to the Sacral chakra. The sacral chakra aids co-creation.

Intuition comes from the color gold. A color related both to the Navel, as well as the Solar Plexus.

When standing on stage to teach, or when counselling or healing, protect your Green Heart by opening your Higher Heart.

There are two types of people when it comes to interaction.

'Attention Direction Self' or 'Attention Direction Others'. 'First Responders' are most likely to be 'Attention Direction Others' people. Selfless and Compassionate, they can often suffer from depleted heart energy which contributes to burnout, depression, and heart attacks.

Every one of us in service to others needs to heal our hearts. Moreover, we need to work, and live, from the SPP Higher Heart Center.

The Thymus Gland as Evolutionary Aid

The Higher Heart chakra, also known as the Thymus Chakra, along with energizing, also activates, the Thymus Gland. The Thymus is an organ of the endocrine system. The Thymus gland is healthy at birth, as indicated by its natural size. Over time the Thymus atrophies, it becomes much smaller. This affects health, together with immunity, because the Thymus is the master gland of the immune system.

The back of the Thymus Gland chakra is said to be home to the 'silver cord'. Our connection with our Soul. Therefore, it could be said to act as the seat of the soul in the physical body.

On the other hand, the Soul also connects with the etheric body at the eighth chakra above the crown. Hence the Soul has dual connection points.

The Thymus works with energy by transmuting it from an electrical impulse into a chemical substance. In other words, the energy is transmuted from the higher levels then stepped down in order that the body can utilize it.

Opening the Higher Heart chakra nourishes the Thymus gland thereby assisting it regain health and size. In the process immunity becomes naturally stronger.

The 'Thymus Thump' is a simple procedure which results in a healthier Thymus gland. Simply tap with the fingers on the surface of the skin over the area of the thymus. See the section on the Thymus Hara Line Chakra for more detailed information

Chapter Review
- The Torus is a Tonal resonator found within male and female electrical paired Spiral Vortices
- The zero point sphere can be used to re-cycle our issues
- We are electrical in nature
- The structure of space or omnipresent stillness, together with the fluctuations of energy within it are the foundation of all our reality. Even the consciousness that animates it.
- We are standing at the brink of this transition from 3D

limitedness to bathing in an infinite amount of energy available everywhere

- To be a full participant you need to align and repair your hara lines, which are an intrinsic part of your energy structure
- We are all connected and unified
- The Higher Heart Chakra (Thymus Chakra) is located in between the green heart and the blue throat chakras. It is dark teal in color
- Use the Thymus thump to aid evolution and enhance immunity
- The Higher Heart can play a role in service to humanity. When we are evolved enough the Higher Heart chakra activates. It then becomes the best chakra through which to relate to the world.
- The Higher Heart Chakra zero point sphere is in fact a Space of Pure Potential that takes us beyond the confines of time and space as it is ubiquitous

CHAPTER 3

FINDING SYSTEMS

*A human being is a part of the whole called by us 'universe', a
part limited in time and space. He experiences himself, his
thoughts and feelings, as something separated from the rest, a
kind of optical delusion of his consciousness. This delusion is
a kind of prison for us, restricting us to our personal desires,
and to affection for a few persons nearest to us. Our task must
be to free ourselves from this prison by widening our circle of
compassion to embrace all living creatures and the whole of
nature in its beauty.*
– ALBERT EINSTEIN

HUMANS FUNCTION BEST as nature intended them to. The 'Grand System' is nature's plan for health at all levels. Individual health in the context of physical, emotional, mental, and spiritual. Collective health in the context of family, tribe, community, nation, world, Earth, atmosphere.

Bees and Synocratic Systems

A good microcosmic example of the Grand System in action is a Beehive. Within the hive each individual bee knows what their role is and carries it out without the 'top down power of Dictatorship.' Indeed, no one individual bee is in charge in the beehive, not even the queen. She just assumes the role of egg layer to ensure the creation of more community members in due course. Yet, each member of the hive knows how to function to allow the hive to both survive and thrive. This form of system is termed Synocratic.

The Macrocosm of the Grand System, along with the microcosm of the beehive, are wonderful examples of the ancient Hermetic Axiom, the Principle of Correspondence, *"That which is below is as that which is above, and that which is above, is as that which is below, for the performance of the miracles of the One thing."* Sometimes shortened to "As above, so below."

Humans function best as nature intended within the Grand System. That is not by using only the mind, which as we have seen can be programmed automatically, unintentionally, but by tapping into the power of the heart's energy. The special space within us which gives us access to intuition, pure perception, and the Universal Mind.

Another example of microcosm and macrocosm would be: every cell in our body knows its role and carries it out without an authority figure telling it what to do.

Figure 15 - The busy microscopic world of a single living cell.
From the animation movie called Inner Life of a Cell.

You are like a cell in the body of humanity. Your heart knows its role.

It will guide you to fulfil that role without an authority telling it what to do. The animation movie called *Inner Life of a Cell*[1] is a fascinating glimpse into the busy microcosmic world of a single cell.

Two Truths

As we now know there are two kinds of truth. Firstly, our personal truth, that which we believe is true because we were witness to it in childhood, especially in the first two years. The truth that was shown to us by carers, parents, significant others, and siblings. The truth which we absorbed due to an innate faith in life as it was being demonstrated to us. This faith, of course, is necessary as a start in life. From the age of two to six the programming continued, this time on a wider scale as we were exposed to a greater number of role models; Kindergarten, neighborhood, religious education, and playground. All of those trusted role models were 'naturally' living life as they had been taught by their trusted role models, generation upon generation.

> Everything can be taken from a man but one thing: the last of the human freedoms - to choose one's attitude in any given set of circumstances, to choose one's own way.
>
> - VICTOR FRANKL

Beliefs are thoughts that are persistent in nature. Plus, as already mentioned our beliefs are causal to our experiences. We just keep thinking them in an automatic fashion. Beliefs are not the enemy; they are just archaic. We are products of what we believe we are. It all starts in the mind. Beliefs were there originally to protect us. If they have ceased to be useful we can un-install them, just as we would old out of date software in our computer.

Remember: Fighting against something gives it energy.

Mother Theresa said, *"I'll never go to an anti-war protest, but I will go to a Peace Protest."* Never engage in a fight with others. To do so will give them and the issue energy.

The 'other truth' is only available to us when we access the Space of

Pure Potential. This truth is the truth of the Grand System. This truth leads us along the path of personal growth and evolution. It is a well-trodden path by some. A never trodden path by others. This book is intended to document how to make the journey along this path. As a natural result you will blend your own personal truth, with the Grand System Truth, enabling you to perceive in a pure way.

I have already covered the need for correcting erroneous perceptions. I will now explain *how* we can correct the movement of erroneous perceptions. When a person has used their unconscious filters like a selective camera lens, to create their own 'internal representation' of their world, this is always based on mis-perceptions, conditioned or copied from role models. In the main, the role models present early in life. However, there may also be strong influencers present during adolescence or adulthood. These erroneous misperceptions connect to, then infect, others in addition to the Earth as well as everything else. It must be remembered how people fit into the natural world, influencing it for good or ill.

We catch misapprehensions like diseases. I'm sure you've heard the old adage 'Assumptions make an ass of u and me.' News that the glass is half empty will travel more quickly than news that it is half full.

Re-write Your Personal History

We can choose to re-write our personal history. Dr. Bruce Lipton maintains that prior to age six we are sponge-like, absorbing the beliefs and values of significant others. We have complete faith in those who bring us up. We have to have this faith. It's a survival strategy. Yet as we age we realize that the faith was sometimes misplaced. When we discover what aspects of our history we wish to re-write, which beliefs limit us, which attitudes are disempowering or which mis-apprehensions we'd rather let go of because they have ceased to serve, then we can do so both quickly and easily.

Here are just a few simple ways the Guides reminded me of that enable a return to balance after impedance of energetic flow through insults, physical injuries, or the mind's negative self-talk.

1. The Breath

Poisons in the air, toxins that impede breath, or things in the person that restrict optimum inhalation or exhalation need to be addressed.

Breathing allows oxygen to be taken up into the blood. Oxygen has a different vibration to carbon dioxide. CO_2 has a lower vibration than O_2. Correct diaphragmatic breathing engenders health. Breathing only in the top of the lungs engenders anxiety. The level of vibration dictates the level of health. Aim to be both a 'Belly Breather' and a 'Chest Breather.' Yoga practice teaches how to belly breathe utilizing the diaphragm. The diaphragm is a muscle that can hold emotion. By breathing deeply, the emotion can be released.

2. Sustenance and Nurturance

We must sustain ourselves through clean, non-toxic, fresh, unprocessed food, devoid of lots of preservatives or pesticides. This together with the loving nurturance of self and others is crucial. If any of these are poor, then the vibration of our being is poor.

The body needs occasional servicing, just like a car. Adequate rest. A diet and environment as free from toxins as possible.

Occasional massage, reflexology, or body work. Heat treatments, such as Sauna or Steam bath. Movement, gentle stretching, or walking. All these activate the natural self-healing and balancing processes, naturally present in each of us.

3. Social Discord

Other people can cause an individual's vibration to reduce. This occurs in all groups of co-operative mammals. Also in communal plants. The homeostatic vibration allows association in groups. For example, if a group of women live together then their menstrual cycles will synchronize. Rhythms synchronize. Entanglement happens. Without flow there is no homeostasis. It is advisable to move away from those who create discord instead of accord.

Emotional Vibrations

E-motion is energy in motion. Remember, energy is a thing when present in the third dimension. You can change an emotional reaction by working with the unconscious mind. You can learn how to do that in the online methodology section. Please understand that emotions, whether you perceive them as good or bad, positive, or negative, are purely information. Education and awareness will raise your EQ (Emotional Quotient). We will attempt through the compassionate sharing of knowledge to assist in raising EQ.

Think of the emotion as a form of email message from your 'Executive Branch', or from another aspect of yourself. You may call it your Higher Self if you wish. If you don't open the inbox, or if you ignore them, the messages stack up. Eventually, you are forced to take notice in the form of a breakdown, an accident, or a major insult to the body on a mental, emotional, or physical level.

It's worth mentioning here that rain in the Savanna initiates a high vibration. Drought a low one. Water is life. Water is the basis of many different bodily forms, as we will discuss next.

Review

- Our unconscious mind is responsible for behavior and operates according to programs until we delete the program
- Perceptions are not pure until we work at removing the impurities or skewed perceptions due to programming
- You can choose to stop being a victim of your own mind. You can use your mind to help or hurt yourself or others
- You can resolve out of sync-ness
- Emotional health, and physical health are inextricably linked
- There exist simple methods of getting unstuck emotionally, physically, mentally, spiritually
- You have Personal Power. You can choose to get it back
- Correct the movement of erroneous debilitating perceptions/ misapprehensions

- The perpetual entanglement of people's energy is a fact of life
- It is paramount that each person creates harmonious inter-actions both with others, and with the Earth
- Remember: The Primary Purpose of the human is to live, learn and grow. Problems occur when any of these is neglected
- The Grand System - nature has a plan and we ignore it at our peril
- The Heart Space or Space of Pure Potential (SPP) within each person is ubiquitous
- Microcosm and macrocosm, the Principle of Correspond-ence; as above so below
- Our goal is pure perception which is our real personal truth

Water

We consist of between 60% and 75% water. Sound affects water. In fact, water has memory. Therefore, instead of 'miracles happening with mind over matter' maybe it should be said, 'mind over water.'

Humans consist mostly of water. Therefore, we can choose to change. We can become what we want to be, because water can become anything. For example, water is the main ingredient in all drinks, it's contained in all foods. All human or animal bodies are over 60% water. Babies up to age one year are over 75% water. The vegetables zucchini, radish and celery comprise 95% water.

How Thoughts Affect Water's Integrity and Structure

A film entitled *Water* was released some years ago. It contained inter-views with internationally based scientists, researchers, clerics, alterna-tive therapists, and Buddhists. It cited many and varied experiments. Research that proved water has memory. Moreover, water can become structured, or unstructured. When structured it is indeed the water of life. We could say Sacred. In this form it may be used to bring healing to the body. Unstructured water, let's term it dead water, brings ill health, even mental instability, insanity, depression, or the loss of the will to live.

> Dr. Emoto's clear vision helps people to see ourselves and our universe otherwise. Science and spirit unite, leading to a profound and plain jump in however we tend to read our world, and the way we are able to reclaim our health and build peace.
>
> — MARCUS LAUX ND

Geopathic stress can affect water for good or ill. Nuclear bombs, hydrogen bombs, both left their 'negative wave residue' in water. Water that affected generations of people and animals, long after the physical evidence of the bomb damage was gone.

The hundredth monkey syndrome[2] could be attributed to water. Furthermore, it has been found that two vessels, each containing a part of the same single sample of water, can interact with each other.

Interesting Facts about Water

DNA is formed from water. The theory is that if the water on the planet is holding a high vibration, via divine grace, and high vibrational messages via word sounds, then humanity will have a consciousness shift. It is said that a few people working together can bring this about. Maybe the energy from solar flares can do it. The research showed that water knew about a big solar flare before it was seen to happen.

It is said that people retain the water of their town of birth throughout their lives even if they drink water from other places. This could explain the phenomena of homesickness or national pride. Drinking water from the birth town can bring back early memories of living there. A folk story tells of a poor shepherd in the 1600's who was orphaned, then taken from his birthplace. During his search for a new country to live in, it is said he found his birthplace again when he drank water from a spring located at his original home co-ordinates.

The so called 'Venezuelan virgin mother water' is rainwater. It is said to be the 'purest water on Earth.' The indigenous people who live in the region consume the water their whole lives. They are said to be amongst the healthiest people on Earth. The people have stated that they do not want civilization to descend on them because that would pollute them, together with their water. Their water is untouched by humans before they drink it.

The only way water cleanses itself of memory is to become evaporated.

In the 1950's a group of people in the process of biological warfare research, died of poisoning. It is said this occurred as a result of drinking the table water provided during the conference. The water was subsequently tested. It was found to be H_2O with no detectable impurities. No other collectively consumed culprit was ever found.

A group of cast away sailors in the 1890's all prayed that the water around them would turn to fresh. It is said that it did, hence they survived for three weeks before they were rescued.

A Chinese Researcher gained the attention of the Chinese government with his new recipe for alternative fuel. He mixed 75% water with 25% diesel then added an emulsifier. This fuel generates 5% more power than normal diesel.

Water burns slowly—it oxygenates.

Heavy water makes hydrogen bombs.

Word of mouth evidence maintains so called 'holy water' from certain shrines has health giving properties.

Love and gratitude are the two words that most positively affect water.

Words create a ripple effect in the same way as a stone thrown into water.

In the movie *What the Bleep Do We Know* we are advised to think of our body as beautiful and send it our gratitude in order to assist it to be healthy. How would you feel if every day, perhaps numerous times a day, you were criticized?

Hidden Messages in Water

The book the *Hidden Messages in Water*[3] became a *New York Times* bestseller. The author, internationally famed Japanese Scientist Masaru Emoto,[4] shows how our thoughts, words, and feelings influence water molecules. It is only a short jump to realize that our thoughts and feelings impact our personal health, other people and the Earth because of the high-water content of people and the planet.

This book has the potential to deeply remodel your perspective so you can realize that victimization is often an inside job.

Dr. Masaru Emoto developed special high-speed photography in freezing cold conditions in order to capture images of ice crystal shapes frozen in water. The crystal shapes change once specific, targeted thoughts are directed toward them.

Figure 16 - Dr. Masaru Emoto developed special high-speed photography in freezing cold conditions in order to capture images of ice crystal shapes frozen in water.

He found that water from pure natural springs and water that has been exposed to positive words show good, cohesive, symmetrical, perfect complex crystalline 'snowflake' patterns. You could call it structured water. On the contrary, impure water, or water exposed to negative thoughts, gives rise to incomplete, asymmetrical patterns or so-called unstructured water.

Figure 17 - The crystal of Sadia Chand's structured and energized water called 'Spirit'.

Electromagnetic radiation is a water de-structuring device. The more metal in a person's body the more susceptible to EMR they are. Vaccines insert aluminum and other heavy metals.

Two Kinds of Emotion

Various emotions, together with where they originate in the body, can be said to be messages.

There are two types of emotion: -

- **Innate native emotions:**
  anger, frustration, envy, hatred, love
- **Societally applied, learned emotions:**
  guilt, judgment, comparing self to others, shame, remorse, resentment

The feelings of remorse or embarrassment offer us a learning moment. In comparison, guilt or shame are designed to disconnect us from our free will.

Some societies do not know guilt or shame; they simply do not have words for these feelings. Judeo Christian ethics to control the masses utilize guilt, shame, or both, very well, in order to undermine or undercut strength and personal power.

A child who is learning to talk will only demonstrate innate, natural emotions. Any emotions a child of that age does not naturally demonstrate are societally applied. They are not an innate human emotion. At around age eighteen to twenty-four months, humans acquire language. However, they *understand* language at around four to five months. They only begin to utilize speech from around eighteen, twenty-four, or thirty months. During early speech development their emotions are innate, unfettered. For example: demanding, I want I want, displaying anger, frustration. At such an early age judging, guilt, comparison, shame, or remorse, is never experienced therefore never demonstrated. You can, however, observe the child demonstrating love, or compassion, for small creatures or soft cuddly toys.

E-motion Is Energy in Motion

John Mc Curdy said, "If I am feeling negative emotion, I am thinking something that isn't true. Period." He went on to say....

"In order to lessen negative emotion in our lives, we must first learn to find the thoughts that are causing the fear, anger or frustration then get better at changing the thoughts. So that the thoughts come up less and less often. Consequently, you feel good more often. It is much easier to monitor your emotions than it is to monitor your thoughts. We have way too many thoughts. Many of them are so habitual, it is hard for us to even catch them on the way through. It just feels normal to think negatively; we have been doing it for so long. I am motivated to change the thoughts by knowing it will make me feel better, rather than worse."

> Feelings are programs; that is, they are learned responses that often have a purpose.
>
> – Dr. David R Hawkins

Emotional health is related to intestinal health. It's not only about changing what you eat. Not wanting to fight with others is an aspect of health. A person who harangues their siblings or intimate partner will undermine the other's well-being.

A truck driver who has just eaten a very high fat breakfast of fried eggs, bacon, sausage, fried tomatoes, fried bread, then rounded it all off with a large cup of coffee, will be placing stress on the liver. The liver, in turn, will make its displeasure felt by generating a feeling of anger in that person. This anger might then be expressed as impatience or road rage, thereby affecting or 'infecting' others.

Emotions are energy. Energy is 'a thing,' energy is 'something' when not in spirit, therefore physical matter is comprised of energy.

Napoleon Hill explored this fact together with the basic connection of mind with reality, in his book *Think and Grow Rich*. He said, "Truly thoughts are things, and powerful things at that, when they are mixed with definiteness of purpose, persistence, and a burning desire for their translation into riches or other material objects." Hill directly correlates the act of thinking about something to the creation of the actual physical reality. Through examples together with quotes, Hill proves the truth of 'thoughts are things.'

Rhonda Byrne, after reading the Wallace D Wattles classic *The Science of Getting Rich*, first published in 1910, wrote *The Secret*, thereby exposing the mainstream media, and consequently the general public, to the idea that thoughts, along with emotions, have vibrational energy. Additionally, that vibrational energy is real, indeed a fact of life. Byrne said "What most people don't understand is that a thought has a frequency. We can measure a thought." The book focuses on one small aspect of the laws of energetic movement, our frequency, and the idea that "thoughts become things."

Action together with reaction, is really what is going on in the energetic world. While we sit alone, we are neither acting nor reacting, there is no flow. We must be out in the world, both acting and reacting with the environment and other people, in order to make energy flow, thereby creating potential for things to be different.

In the 1961 book, *The Law and the Promise*, Neville suggests that we are affected not only by the world, but also the thoughts and the energy of the people around us. It is the vibrations or expectations of those near us that can alter our vibrations, or vice versa. In other words, we get what we think we will get. Neville suggests that if we just alter our thought or attitude about a thing, then the thing will change. Neville claims this is the key to change. He also states that if we alter our own thoughts, we also allow others to alter their thoughts.

That is to say, by our own change, we can help change other people's thoughts about us.

A facilitator must be careful of personal attitude when helping others change because of the possibility of potentially limiting others by what we personally believe they can achieve. We can, with our thoughts or expectations, affect the actions or the behaviors of all others in our world.

In the world of Quantum Physics, this phenomenon of thought has the potential to alter the physical world, is very well known. The theory is that in observing, one changes or adds to the action or movement of the energy simply by observing or expecting a specific outcome. In other words, Quantum Physics has documented that observation, human expectations, and thought, are proven to make changes in the physical world.

Traditional Chinese medicine (TCM) speaks of meridians in the body that function as channels to allow the energy to flow. TCM doctors focus on ensuring the energy can flow unimpeded. The specific Traditional Chinese Medicine methods of Acupuncture, Acupressure and Shiatzu are used to unblock energy channels. A fundamental notion of TCM is the prevention of disease together with the maintenance of health. Historically, a TCM Doctor was paid a retainer to keep their patients healthy. If a patient became sick, the doctor would not be paid again until the patient's health returned. In a similar vein, a doctor that resorted to surgery was considered an inferior doctor. It is thought that if he or she had done their job correctly, their patients would have remained healthy. There would be no need to perform invasive surgery.

The Natural Disruption of Energy

There are three ways to disrupt the flow of energy in the body

1. Through the Mind (via thoughts or inner dialogue)
2. Through Physical injuries (when injuries fail to heal well it is due to emotional components in conflict with healing)
3. Through Emotional injuries (I call these 'insults')

A young mind certainly prior to age six or seven, is very malleable so emotional injuries only occur when the experience elicits a strong, serious, aggravated, emotional response (i.e. parental fights, acute danger, intense fear, wartime experiences, ritual or systematic abuse). Otherwise the child will not absorb the emotional issues. As we mature, we become more aware of the external three-dimensional world, less focused inward. As a result, insults, betrayal being the most commonplace, are experienced. These experiences elicit a primal or primate type response, which is 'me first, you second.'

Betrayal is perceived as – I'm not as important as you are. You do not value me as much as you value yourself.

The Most Common Emotions That Lodge in the Body's Field

Anger: perceived as – you are trespassing against me, my ego, or my interests. Or trespassing against those I care about.

Frustration: perceived as – I am impeded from receiving what I want or attaining my goals.

Shame/Guilt is invented by others to diminish or reduce personal power. The personal inner perception therefore becomes – 'I am not worthy.'

Remorse is communal – I understand my actions were incorrect. I sincerely wish to change them.

The three most diminishing are shame, guilt, or betrayal, because in addition, they cause feelings of *fear*.

Fear is related to: I perceive danger, to me, mine, or my community. I fear not having enough: food, money, love. I fear an imminent threat to me or a danger to my livelihood.

How do these responses cause insults, followed by a consequential change in energetic flow?

Let me repeat: Emotions are energy. Energy comprises 'some-thing' when on the earth plane.

Emotions, or Emotional incidents, lodge within the body. They stay there forever until they are released or resolved. Release or resolution can only happen after agreement has been reached between mind and body.

When emotions are experienced as a result of an event, or experiences are created, there is always a reason, a lesson to be learned. Or a belief that this, whatever it is, is needed in some way. Simply put we have chosen or commanded it. Accepting that this is true is a challenge for most people. It results in our needing to accept responsibility. Remember we project what we perceive through the unconscious mind. We see 'out there' the results of our own creativity. We live in a personal universe within the greater common Universe. No one else shares our personal version of 'reality.'

We are creating each experience whether we know it or not. Whether consciously, or not. In order to 'cleanly create' it is necessary to fully appreciate the power of the mind over the body. Fire walking or lying on a bed of nails are good examples of the power of the mind. Additionally, how much power the mind has over energy is extremely important.

Remember some of the prime directives of the unconscious mind that operate within this context are:

- to be a servant, to follow orders
- to generate as well as transmit energy
- to take everything personally.

Therefore, to build rapport with the mind, to gently tame, and calm the mind, is the way to the purest of perception. Hence it is the way to the purest, best health.

It is possible to change anything that is stored as a memory because it is stored holographically.[5] The unconscious mind is responsible for the organization and storage of memories and internal representations. Emotions are a component of a memory, along with the visual, auditory, kinesthetic, olfactory, gustatory information. Add to that the thoughts or self-talk being generated at the time. We can release the emotional component of a memory, while retaining the memory. Consequently, we can recall the event, yet we remain in an emotionally neutral state.

David Hawkins in his book *Pathway of Surrender* has said, "Repressed and suppressed feelings require counter-energy to keep them submerged. It takes energy to hold down our feelings. As these feelings are relinquished, the energy that had been holding down the negativity is now freed for constructive uses."

In the same book David also wrote about how the body can communicate with us through muscle testing (kinesiology). He said, "If you think a guilty thought and have somebody test your muscle strength, you will see that the muscle instantly goes weak. Your cerebral hemisphere has become de-synchronized and all of your energy meridians are thrown out of balance. Nature, therefore, says that guilt is destructive."

Away from or Towards Motivation

We have all experienced the feeling of being motivated. Have you ever stopped to consider whether you are keen to get towards something, or away from it? Is it fear that drives you, or the excitement of improving your life?

There are more people who are motivated by needing to get away from the object of their fear. This causes an inner conflict within the unconscious mind due to the fact that the unconscious is both the home of the imagination, and the core means of goal achievement. Remember that the unconscious mind cannot process the word *not* as we discussed earlier. When you add imagination, inability to process the negated instruction, and goal achievement ability, together, you realize that if you are persistently thinking of the fear, and creating internal visuals of the fear, then the goal seeker within you will seek the fear rather than what you want. Don't think of a pink elephant. What do you see on your inner screen? I rest my case.

Assess Towards or Away From Motivation

If you are seeking wealth because you fear not having enough money you will sabotage yourself. My own experience twenty years ago taught me the importance of towards motivation. My NLP trainer asked me "why do you want to make money?" My reply was "because I don't want to live in a cardboard box on the street."

*Figure 18 – Is your motivation generally towards what you want,
or away from what you want to avoid?*

He said, "Ah, you have an 'away from' motivation for making money. Have you ever considered changing that?" "I'd love to", I said, "because I'd like to make money in order to fulfil my life purpose of helping others and teaching them how to use their minds resourcefully. I want to open a training academy." Within one year I had built the classroom as an extension to my home and run my first training course. I doubt that would have happened if my 'away from living on the street' had remained in my consciousness.

SPP, Healing Power, Zero, Templates and Scalar Waves

The Space of Pure Potential (SPP), as I have said, is an energetic area in the upper chest near to the physical heart but not part of it. Nor is it part of the green heart chakra. It is a place that lies beyond the space time continuum. It gives us access to zero point scalar energy waves in the center of the zero point sphere of the higher heart. It is a place that allows us to experience trust. It is where enlightenment lives. It's a vast ubiquitous openness that interconnects us to everything else that exists. It's a Pure Potential Energy Zero Point Sphere in our body, our access to All That Is, where the infiniteness of universe, along with the infiniteness of human, interact. It's a point of entry, gateway or portal, into infiniteness.

Scalar Waves

Scalar waves are the means by which thought creates. A Scalar pattern, or grid, is created by a thought or an idea. Scalar is Light and sound technology. Scalar Waves are standing waves of energy that create a morphogenetic field (aka electromagnetic grid). They flash on and off. When 'on' they are in the mode of fission. When 'off' they are in fusion mode. In very simple terms fission creates and fusion integrates.

A thought or an idea gives rise to a scalar pattern. A scalar pattern gives rise to a template which becomes the causal factor beneath all manifestations of physicality in all dimensional expression. Humans emit internally generated scalar waves naturally.

Equipment to emit them for both energy generation and medical use has been around since Tesla,[6] and he died in 1943. During the 1960's and 70's the Frenchman Antoine Poire furthered Tesla's original work. More recently Meyl's[7] research in Europe and Tom Bearden's efforts in the USA has brought Scalar technology to the forefront once again. Unfortunately, these days the technology has been weaponized into what is termed 'Scalar Pulse Frequency Weapons.'

Our thoughts and feelings have an electromagnetic reality. Manifest wisely.

– RITA MARR

The amazing truth is that we, as humans, are natural generators and emitters of scalar waves. We can do this on demand using the power of our intention. Scalar waves are the means by which creation happens on a personal or multi-versal scale. They form the Templates for existence.

Templates

How does Spirit become matter? Templates are the means whereby matter is created out of spirit or electrical energy (Figure 19).

Templates are created from Scalar Standing Waves that form grids or matrices. The Scalar Waves are created from the smallest units of consciousness called Partiki.[8] You could say the Partiki is the much sought after 'God Particle.' The Template for the human body gives rise to the human. A distorted template gives rise to a distorted human. A perfect Divine Blueprint gives rise to the original human as originally created. The Template may become distorted due to events, insults, genetic engineering, or genealogical limitations inherent in the DNA. We can choose to repair and regenerate the distorted Template in order to heal, evolve our consciousness and increase our light quotient. Our goal is to return to our original divine blueprint.

There is so much I'd like to share about the nature of the myriad of specific Templates utilised for creation in general, and for our bodies in particular, however it's beyond the scope of this book. My next book perhaps.

Partiki

As I have said Partiki[9] could be said to be the 'God particle' that Quantum Physicists seek.

Because it is not physical they will not find it. More accurately Partiki are the waves of God thought or intention. According to Keylonta Science, the Akasha and Universal Physics, it is the first act of creation from our Divine God Source Eternal Supreme One. Partiki are Primal Energy Units of Ante-Matter (precede matter) that stem from sound (frequency/vibration) as the 'intention' of Source. They divide into mated pairs of opposites.

Partiki as ante-matter have the ability to create both matter and its paired opposite, anti-matter. Partiki split into two mated polarities, or fields, in the act of fission. On one side Particum create the Universe where we have our existence. On the other side Partika give rise to the dark (anti) matter universe. Partika and Particum are the building blocks of creation.

Anti-matter is the other side of the mirror to our reality. Here left becomes right and right becomes left. My Guides call it Dark Matter, the Mirror or the parallel Universe. Dark Matter is a substance that is unseen, yet it creates an effect on matter. The Dark Matter universe is opposite in expression from our Universe. Creator then pulls these two units back into Itself in an act of fusion to become its original Omi-Polar, Ante-matter Partiki unit. Hence the flashing on and off cycle.

Zero – Is It a Dangerous Number?

In Newtonian physics zero implies stationary, no movement. In the quantum world zero is a place where *all* energy exists. Zero[10] is a paradox that threatens science. Zero is infinity's twin.

The void and infinity can be equated. Zero is the language of nature. The Greeks embraced abstract philosophy yet never discovered zero. The concept of the zero came from the East, from Babylon, it was the Babylonians who discovered the placeholder system. The battles over the zero, shook science, mathematics, and religion. Zero shook humanity's view of God and the Universe.

When you consider the numbers 1, 2, 3, 4, 5, 6, 7, 8, and 9 there is of course, no zero on the number line.

Some then put the zero before the 1. The Mayans put the zero after 9. The Greeks despised the zero even though they acknowledged its usefulness. The Greeks knew zero links to the void. They had a primal fear of chaos and the void. Other cultures were equally fearful of the concept of the void or chaos. The ancient Sanskrit Vedas[11] on the other hand taught neither space nor sky, nor existence nor non-existence was to be feared.

In the 9th Century BC in India both Hindus and Buddhists came up with the idea of personal transcendence over the natural world by reaching an emptiness in the mind. They termed it Samadhi—a place of consciousness yet absence of thought.

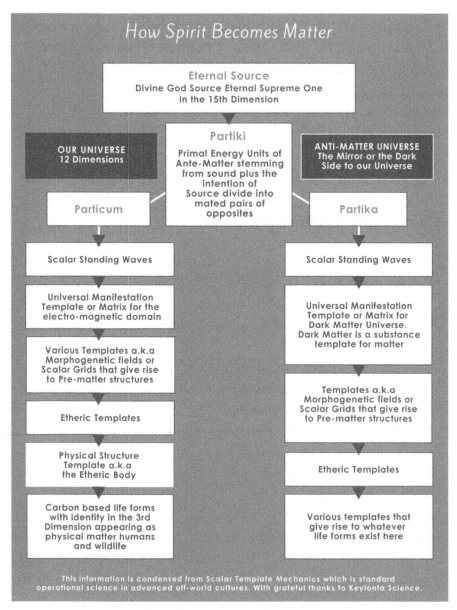

Figure 19 – How energy becomes matter.

It took until the 16th Century AD for the concept of zero to reach

Europe. When it did the 'Age of Reason' took the zero and placed it before the one. And oh dear!! Materialism ran with an erroneous idea. An illogical but convenient concept that was completely misunderstood both in that time, and later by Isaac Newton. The Eastern scholars placed the 0 after 9. Conversely the Merchants of the West used it before the one. Because of the use of 0 in the context of nothing exists there in a material sense, it caused chaos in mathematics, religion and science, because in fact there cannot be no-thing there!

The mercantile impulse caused the erroneous use of zero and after that came the rejection of spirituality and the divorce of science and mathematics from spirituality.

Here is an example of zero at work:

$$3 + 0 = 3$$
$$3 - 0 = 3$$
$$3 \times 0 = 0$$

3 divided by 0 = ?? Chaos!! Not allowed, because this cannot be answered.

In mathematics division by zero was conveniently banned in order that all theorem could be accepted as true. Of course, in truth all theorem was flawed—including Newton's calculus which was written with a rider that said, "excluding division by zero."

How typically human to be arrogant enough to say something that is against natural law is true, simply because the human mind cannot conceive of the truth, or does not want to accept the truth, of the creation story. Ignoring something just because it will challenge existing beliefs, or fashionable thinking, is an arrogant de-volutionary egoic trait. Typical of reduced consciousness.

Because of this, mathematically, zero is excluded or banned.

The infinite density of the zero point sphere is a division by zero.

Space or omnipresent stillness is a zero.

Pythagoras was unaware of zero. Logic reigned during his time.

Order, predictability, and rational thought were all possible before the concept of zero. Zero implied the existence of a Creator God. That cannot be rationalized!

Empirical observation, rather than philosophy, therefore came into dominance.

Everyone can access this space of omnipresent stillness within. The zero point sphere of the higher heart. The SPP. Most people have to learn how to do that on demand. Everyone has experienced being in the SPP spontaneously.

For example, we touch into it each time we feel really loved; when we gaze at a newborn child; when we take in the sheer beauty of nature, or after the loving intimacy of coitus.

Just think of what you adore. Think of it bubbling up joy within you. You effortlessly move into the SPP. Engage with something you love to do, and hey presto, you are in SPP.

To define this place, which lies beyond the space time continuum, let me use the concept of the Stepping Stones analogy given by the Guides.

The Moment of Suspension Concept – the Zero Point Moment

Stepping Stones analogy: Imagine you are walking along a row of stepping stones. As you step onto the next stone the previous one disappears. In the space between the disappearance of the old stone and the creation of the new, whilst the foot is in the air, there is a moment we shall call the 'moment of suspension.' This moment holds infinite possibilities.

In four legged animals this moment occurs as they change from using the front two legs to using the back two legs as they move. There is a continual switching.

The more we believe anything is possible when in this 'moment of suspension' the more encompassing the change.

The Healer can use the 'moment of suspension' to induce lightning fast change in the subject. If the subject can also move into that moment through spoken guidance, and 'allowing' (as a skill), then the change is blessed with more gracefulness. The 'moment of suspension' is a moment of trust. It is the access point to 'Pure Potentiality.' 'Pure Potentiality' is the moment in time that the highest degree of expansion and healing can occur.

The Space of Pure Potential
Helps You Be the Best Healer You Can Be

My task, through my teachings is firstly to introduce you to the concept, then secondly, to better understand the nature, of the place within you I call the Space of Pure Potential (SPP).

When we as humans connect into both the non-dimensional Eternal Source of All That There Is (ATTI), Divine God Source Eternal Supreme One, First Cause, and the Earth, then, in addition, make an agreement to release an issue, our intention together with the breath enables the release. If the healing recipient is not connected to ATTI and the Earth but the Practitioner/Facilitator offering the healing is, plus the Healer is in their SPP, then the release will happen. This is because the Practitioner is acting as the means by which an issue can move through the third dimension, into no dimension, in order to release it. So now we are beginning to understand why some healers are more effective than others. It's a matter of connectedness. If the hara lines of the healer are weak, in need of alignment, functioning at less than optimal levels, then the Healing power together with the effect, will be compromised.

How can an issue move through the third dimension into no dimension in order to be released?

Let's explain by using the box analogy.

The Box Analogy

If we take a box as a cube to represent third dimensional defined energy, then when we collapse the box flat, into a plane, it represents undefined energy moving from 3D to 2D. In theory it may then also move to 1D if we could shrink it into a tiny speck. Then on to no dimension, when the speck blows away into freedom. When a 3D issue reaches no-dimension it ceases to be. Therefore, as facilitators we just need to encourage people to let this happen energetically. Connection, together with natural normal breathing, allows the issue to go free.

Position in the Body of the Zero Point Sphere

However, it's not as simple as just entering the zero point sphere of the higher heart. The place of the zero point is slightly different in each person because sometimes the person is 'out of body' due to fears or challenging emotional residue. There is another field that is used when the person is outside of their body. Describing this field is beyond the scope of this book.

The Zero Point Sphere or SPP can be outside of a person if that person is not in their center or not in their body because they feel uncomfortable about being fully present in the third dimensional physicality.

Sometimes the discomfort is due to porous energy bodies, or wide-open unaffiliated chakras. Unaffiliated chakras are extremely open. Therefore, they are able to absorb the energy in the immediate environment which is outside of the person's own energy field. For example, fifty per cent of the population have a very open solar plexus chakra by design, it enables them to be very empathetic. They are able to absorb low and high vibrational bio-magnetic energy from other people which they then have to process as if it belongs to them. It is unfortunate that they easily absorb electro-magnetic energy from the environment as well, which can cause discomfort and dis-ease.

Before any release can occur, it is necessary for the person to be in their center before they begin the process of getting into their SPP. Also it's useful if the person knows whether or not they have a particularly porous energy system or field.

A person needs to be fully in body, fully 'home' in order to be healthy. Becoming comfortable, 'at home' as it were, is a prerequisite for getting into and staying in the SPP. There are a large number of people who are uncomfortable in their bodies. They are continually trying to get away from themselves. This creates spaces in the energy field, in subtle bodies, which can then be filled, or used by, energies we would prefer to remain free of. I call these entities hangers on, hitchhikers or parasites.

Systems and Fractals

I hope that I have given you enough evidence of the essential interconnectedness and interdependence with all life. It is a fact that if we see ourselves as separate then we will suffer ill health.

Truth Unites Us – Lies and Deceit Separate Us

We all know that unsustainability will result if the current destructive actions of humanity continue. Full entropy will be the result. Many communities have destroyed themselves in the past.

Since we are so interconnected, we will destroy ourselves if we continue without change.

The separate notes of the piano keys are made into music by co-operation, by the player or players creating tuneful chords. A concerto is a 'concerted' effort, a team effort each aspect being of equal importance.

Systems

It is important to acknowledge the essential interconnection and interdependence between all life everywhere. We should perceive 'Holistic (Wholistic) Units' consisting of all of us together, rather than perceiving oneself as an individual unit, part or bit. The key to world peace is the contagion of love and connectedness through community.

When projecting a hologram[12] the whole item can be projected by shining a coherent light (laser) through only one small piece of the whole. Holograms are excellent proof of the whole being completely present in each and every part of the whole. In addition, if you make a change in one piece then that change is immediately reflected in the hologram of the whole.

Understanding the nature of systems is key to understanding the nature of this book.

Fractals

All energy is fractal in nature. A copy of a pattern. A repeat, of a repeat, of a repeat, of a pattern.

In a Fractal the smallest portion is repetitive to the grandest portion – all pieces of a fractal are connected. A snowflake is a good example of a fractal. A fractal is a good example of a repetitive system.

Let's take the following example of a snowflake pattern.

Before iterating[13] a single triangle.

Repeat the triangle five times.

Repeat this pattern five times.

Figure 20 - Snowflakes are fractal in nature.

Repeat over and over. Eventually the familiar snowflake[14] pattern appears.

Review

- There are two kinds of emotion, Innate. Societally applied
- E-motion is energy in motion
- Natural disruption of energy occurs in three ways; through the mind; through physical injuries; through emotional injuries
- Both 'Away From' and 'Towards' motivation exist
- A Space of Pure potential exists in every person yet the Zero Point sphere of the heart is positioned slightly different if the person is 'out of body'
- Scalar waves are created by all living things. They carry information and constitute templates. They are created from Partiki and its mated opposites Particum and Partika
- Zero is a powerful number
- The moment of suspension enables instant change to take place
- Transmuting issues from 3D to no dimension - the box analogy
- Systems – the key to world peace is the contagion of love and connectedness through community.
- All energy is Fractal in nature

CHAPTER 4

FINDING HEALTH

If humans were to model the lifestyle displayed by a healthy community of cells, our societies and our planet would be more peaceful and vital.
— DR. BRUCE LIPTON

INSULTS & PIVOT POINTS are terms you will become familiar with as you read on. In short, a Pivot Point is a quick change of direction. Just like when a dancer 'pivots.' More about that later. An insult is anything that impacts or changes the healthy, normal, function or flow of a system. A system can be as small as a single cell. A collection of cells, as in the nervous system. A combination of systems, as in the human. Or as large as Earth. Or larger, ad infinitum. The solar system being an example.

Insults & Pivot Points

An insult can affect a single specific system of the body or generally effect all systems. Cancer affects all systems right up to and including the structural level. As an aside here, let me mention how some time ago I began to consider what if some incidents of cancer could manifest as a result of an insult that caused stagnation? In other words, lack of energetic flow. What if healing could begin to occur if flow returns to areas previously affected by stagnation? Just like removing a tourniquet enables blood to flow again. If the tourniquet remained the area deprived of blood would deteriorate. Dr. Bruce Lipton has stated that "cancer is due to not living in harmony." When we are in harmony, there are naturally less insults, energy flows more easily, and homeostasis is supported. As I was writing this section, I was pleased to get even further confirmation as I listened to USA based Cancer Specialist Dr. Rashid Buttar DO., FAAPM., FACAM., FAAIM of the Center for Advanced Medicine being interviewed. He clearly stated that he believes that cancer is caused by lack of energy flow and lowered energy levels.

A repeated emotional storm can create an insult. Let's take anger for example, as an insult. Anger firstly affects the energy flow of the system. Then it affects the nervous system. Then the Digestive system. Then the circulatory system, and ends up compromising the Heart chakra.

Eating toxic unhealthy food or breathing unclean air or coming in contact with dangerous industrial or domestic chemicals are also insults to the system.

The Health of the Individual Affects All Others in the System

In systems there is natural dependency. For example, the health of many of the animals in the Serengeti can be affected if one predator in the system behaves differently to how nature intended. Humanity is a big system that comprises a number of smaller systems.

Each person is part of a family group which is part of a larger system we can call the socio-economic group, which in turn is a part of the political sector. Health at all levels affects the health in each level. We do not ascribe to alter geopolitical functioning as a whole, we want to assist individuals regain their health and well-being because it is they, in turn, who will affect the health of the entire system. Therefore, gradually, one person at a time becoming energetically healthy means there is less discord in the system. All individual units must be functioning in a respectful healthy manner in order to support the whole.

Here's another example. Let's say a country has a volatile angry Dictator as a leader, who has a tendency to suffer digestive issues. Digestive issues in turn contribute to exacerbated feelings of anger, which then affects the liver function. When this occurs anger will tend to be very strongly and overtly expressed to all those around. Therefore, his subjects directly or indirectly eventually become poisoned by the anger. Eventually the entire wholeness the leader exerts power over, which in this case of course is their country, suffers just because of one person's ill health.

System health is vitally important. Especially in families or in relationships. Health or illness is equally infectious! Whiners negatively affect the energy of those within hearing distance. The health of the human in relation to the others in their lives will be addressed within this book. Office employee groups are like small tribes or families in that they can infect or affect each other. Females are generally more sensitive to group discord. Homosexual males can be similarly sensitive. Heterosexual males are less so.

Systems of One to Another

In simple terms outside influences affect us. On a global scale let's use the example of mainstream media reporting extreme examples of acts of aggression that trigger shock or horror in the viewers. The influence can also be small. For example, a single gesture, a word, or one person's perception that they share with others in a small group. It only takes two humans to make a fight!

When people share with others a negative experience, or a bad day, this can bring down the vibrationary rate of those who are the recipients of the sharing. In healthier humans there is less tendency to share the negative. The positive is shared instead. We need more sharing of goodness. Less of its opposite.

Pivot Points

A change of belief, or an altered perception that occurs very quickly as a result of a one-off experience, I call a Pivot Point. When a person moves from a blinkered view to a wider view, they have experienced a Pivot Point. Suddenly they see other possibilities. Other ways to react to the same stimulus. A Pivot Point can be brought about simply by another person asking, "have you ever thought of it another way?" In NLP the act of changing perception is called a 'reframe.' A reframe occurs after a Pivot Point has been experienced.

Let's discuss Pivot Points in relation to systems.

Reframes

If another person causes someone to change their perception or belief by asking a question such as "have you ever thought of it this way?" in terms of NLP we have initiated either 'a meaning reframe' or a 'context reframe.' A meaning reframe is where the same behavior suddenly develops a different meaning. An example would be, "I remember my parents deserting me on the beach when I was seven years old. I was devastated. Five minutes later as I was tearfully walking back to our hotel, I saw Dad's car in the beach car park. I realized they were waiting for me all along. I just hadn't heard them calling me." Suddenly the same behavior was seen differently. It meant there was no desertion.

An example of a context reframe example would be if a seven-year-old says, "We were planning a picnic. I'm angry it's raining. It's not fair!"

The child's father, who is a farmer, says, "Well I'm glad it's raining because we've had a long period of drought. I was scared we would lose our farm and our income which would have meant no more picnics ever."

In the *Biology of Belief* Dr. Bruce Lipton covers in detail how belief changes cause actual changes in a human system's biology, cells or even in the DNA. Dr. Lipton has examined in great detail the processes by which cells receive information. The implications of this research radically change our understanding of life. It shows that genes and DNA do not control our biology; that instead DNA is controlled by signals from outside the cell, including the energetic messages emanating from our positive or negative thoughts. His research proves that our bodies can change due to the re-training of our thinking.

Dr. Lipton went on to say, "We need to move beyond Darwinian Theory, which stresses the importance of individuals, to one that stresses the importance of the community." British scientist Timothy Lenton provides evidence that evolution is more dependent on the interaction among species, than it is on the interaction of individuals within a species. Evolution becomes a matter of the survival of the fittest groups rather than the survival of the fittest individuals. In a 1998 article, in the publication *Nature*, Lenton wrote that rather than focusing on individuals, or their role in evolution "we must consider the totality of organisms *and* their material environment to fully understand which traits come to persist and dominate."

Cancelling out the Pattern of the Problem

The antidote to the client's problem will be a healing vibration that will cancel out the pattern of the problem. In essence a pathway needs to be found through which we may work at speed with light, color *and* intention in order to release the problem.

It's worth reiterating that all is energy and energy can be influenced, or tainted, by thought or belief.

We learn to survive regardless of our challenges. Sometimes our survival strategy is resourceful. Other times less so. Like when we wall off a section of life—like a tree grows around obstacles that get in its way. Compartmentalization is unresourceful. According to my NLP Trainer Tad James, the unconscious mind works at its optimum when it is integrated.

This means without walls, without 'Parts' that split off then go their own way with their own agenda. An agenda that is contrary to the agenda of the wholeness of mind. When a client says, "Part of me wants to change, yet there seems to be a part of me resisting change," it is an indicator of lack of wholeness. In such a case, the recalcitrant Part needs to be integrated into the wholeness, before the healing intervention takes place, or there will be resistance. The Part may avoid responding during the healing experience. This means that however hard you work at changing, or healing, the issue will return sooner or later. The Part will become active again and consequently it will re-ignite the issue.

As Healers let's look at some common issues that our clients may present with.

Imbalances Within the Body

Where there are general fears we could ask:

1. What is your biggest fear in life?
2. What do you worry will happen if you do not attend to this fear / frustration?
3. What would your life be like if this issue were gone?

Frustration or Anger

We could ask:

1. What is your biggest frustration in life? Or, what triggers your anger?
2. What do you worry will happen if you do not attend to this frustration or anger?
3. What would your life be like if this issue were gone?

The questions elicit the specific issue, the motivation to release it, and create a future vision of life without the issue. The nervous system is activated where the issue is being held. The problem is loosened up.

It will be easier to release it. I sometimes feel I am aiming at a target. In order to help the person release the issue, I have to hit the center of the bull's eye. If I am off even slightly, then the release is less effective.

Fibromyalgia

Often, Fibromyalgia is related to the following belief system: "I must help people by collecting their garbage. I'm in service to others." In addition, toxic thoughts can also create fibromyalgia. Especially thoughts or inner dialogue along the lines of: "I am a diminished soul. I don't deserve what I want."

Diabetes and Obesity

Diabetes or obesity are often triggered by a perceived lack of love. The reasons may be as follows:

- Fear of lack of love.
- Fear of not having enough love.
- Fear of theft of the love I have (someone may take the love I am currently receiving)
- Fear of loss of my control over myself if I love them or they love me
- Prior trauma / insults (I allowed love and got hurt)
- A belief that I could never have love or be deserving of it.

Diabetes occurs when there is not enough insulin to metabolize the glucose in the food we eat. The sugar then is excreted in the urine rather than transformed into the energy we need. This inability to use the sweetness in the food is reflected in an inability to accept the sweetness of real love. Therefore, diabetes can be related to either a lack of sweetness in life, often because of loss, or loneliness in adults, or an abundance of sweetness, as may be the case in 'smother love' as children.

If we feel undernourished emotionally it can trigger adult onset diabetes to occur. Diabetics often feel isolated and unable to give of themselves. Or they lose their sense of independence due to their reliance on external insulin supplies. Learning to love oneself, together with allowing love to flow from you to others, and vice versa, is crucial.

Obesity can also sometimes be linked with lack of love or a fear of intimacy. We attempt to make up for lack of love nourishment by putting too much food nourishment into our bodies. Or we perceive the need to cushion ourselves against the nasty world out there.

Hypoglycemia occurs if blood sugar drops. This can be linked to having given too much of ourselves to others, yet not enough to self. In which case time is needed to replenish. Also, low blood sugar can occur when there is an over desire for affection or a constant need for outside reassurance.

According to Vicky Wall, the Founder of *Aura Soma*,[1] the spleen transforms substances from the astral body to the etheric body. Emotions enter the physical body via the etheric subtle body. Certain emotions tend to rest in, or have an affinity with, certain parts of the physical body.

For example:

- Bitterness in the bones
- Anxiety in the intestines or stomach
- Anger in the heart, lungs or solar plexus

Let's discuss why this is the case.

Anger Is about Need

Anger is particularly contagious and poisonous because anger is about need. If a person feels powerful, they will never get angry at anyone else. Only when in a state of perceived powerlessness do we generate anger. If someone perceives there is an authority over them, it triggers anger.

The large area, or plane, where anger is commonly held, is the area between the upper thoracic (clavicle) and the top of the diaphragmatic arch.

Within this area, the heart, lungs, and solar plexus are located. The chest area is where we often think of ourselves as residing. We often place our hand on our chest and say 'me.' The chest links to the concept of I, me, mine, selfishness. You have trespassed against me. Anger promulgates lack of compassion, generosity or joining. Anger (also known as wrath) is mentioned as one of the seven deadly sins. Anger rests where the truest self is, in other words in the heart or the solar plexus. Whether it's in the heart or the solar plexus depends on our evolutionary level.

Bitterness and Anger

The liver is affected by both bitterness and anger combined because the liver meridian passes by the location of the physical heart. The liver meridian is in the plane across the body where the heart and liver are located.

Trepidation, Fear, Anxiety

Trepidation or fear is held in the extremities. The head is included as an extremity. A numbness of the mind, or mind fog, can occur. Numbness can also occur in the fingers or toes. 'Fear of being killed' starts in the extremities but affects entire body. In the unfortunate event that we live in terror the entire body is affected. Anxiety or fear also affects the intestines. Trepidation is the fear of moving forward. The hands or feet commonly reflect this.

I should stress at this point that there is no one answer for everything.

Fear caps the mind. Poor decision-making results. Stereotypic behavior occurs. When we are under the effect of fear, we cannot access leadership qualities, therefore we just become group members. Fear based behavior, driven by instinct, or lacking in reason, tends to be illogical. Therefore, most often poor decision-making results.

Responsibility, Guilt, Shame

Responsibility, together with the attendant feelings of guilt, shame, a sense of being over-burdened, or living for others, rather than self, can manifest in the area around the shoulders, the thyroid, down the spine, and into the pancreas. An example would be a mother who feels useless when her children are grown or leave home. She has trouble finding her true identity and balance again because she has been playing the 'mother role' for a long time. Insulin, for example, enables balance in both the body and the thyroid. Guilt, shame or over responsibility, can rest in all places where energy is balanced in the body. For example, across the back, shoulders, or around the hips or endocrine system in the sacral area.

The strength of the human is the shoulders. The shoulders and back reflect a sense of a weighty load of guilt. For example, "I couldn't possibly do that I'd feel too guilty." The low back and hips also can reflect a sense of a heavy load where there is guilt present.

The pancreas is affected if a person is a 'rescuer' who is overly responsible for others, or for their own material belongings.

Expecting love from another to make our pain go away engenders self-rejection.

An Endocrine System imbalance can also occur when these emotions are held onto. Sugar problems (getting energy to nerves and muscles), or digestive system problems, may develop. This occurs especially in submissive types of people. This of course affects relationships.

Layers of Issues

There can be many layers to an issue. For example, layer one: *guilt*. Layer two: *shame*. Layer three: *not speaking one's truth*. Layer four: *not walking one's talk*. Layer five: *not connecting with who one really is or honoring oneself*. Relationship issues often result. I always discover the order in which the layers need to be released. If the order is incorrect then healing is compromised.

Stress

The source of all stress is, unrealized expectation. For example, if your expectation is to drive uncongested roads, stress occurs in busy road conditions.

Relationship and Communication Issues

Relationship and/or communication issues, reflect in the thyroid / neck / upper back area. If we are not walking in our truth, that will show up in the lower back and hips. Different degrees of lack of communication affect us in different ways.

Diverticulitis

Diverticulitis is reminding us that it is time to unwind. Intestinal problems can reflect perfectionism, judgment, a strong 'inner critic,' or the suppression of feelings.

Women and Men in Community

It is a fact that women in community operate differently to men in community. For example, in the case of fraternity the community is only as strong as the connections. Some men can be empathetic to the extent of dying for each other, as is often seen in a theater of war. Women in community, are more likely to be quicker to turn on one another than men, especially in the context of competition for a mate.

Let us recap the section where we discussed the flow of energy in the body.

There are three ways to disrupt the flow:

1. Mind (thoughts or inner dialogue)
2. Physical injuries (when injuries fail to heal well it's due to emotional components being involved)
3. Emotional injuries

A young mind, especially prior to age seven, is very malleable so emotional injuries only occur when the experience elicits a strong, serious, aggravated, emotional response. For example, fights between parents. Real or perceived danger. Fears. Traumatic experiences. War zone events. Otherwise the child will not absorb the emotional issues. As we mature, we become more aware of the outside, third dimensional world, and less focused inward. Hence insults, betrayal being the most commonplace, are experienced. These experiences elicit a primal, or primate type, response, which is 'me first, you second.'

The most common emotions that lodge in the field of the body are anger or frustration.

Betrayal is perceived as: I'm not as important as you are. You do not value me as much as you value yourself.

Anger is perceived as: you are trespassing against me, i.e. my ego, or my interests. Or trespassing against those I care about.

Frustration is perceived as: I am impeded from receiving what I want or attaining my goals.

Shame/Guilt is invented by others to diminish or reduce personal power. The perception here is, I am not worthy.

Remorse is communal. I understand my actions were incorrect. I sincerely wish to change them.

One of the most diminishing emotions is shame, quickly followed by guilt or betrayal. These three often create associated fear around them, so that we end up with fear sitting on top of shame, guilt, or betrayal. In other words, there is a sense of 'I perceive danger, to me, mine or my community.'

'I Fear not having enough food, money and/or love.' 'I fear an imminent threat or danger to my livelihood.'

How do these responses cause insults and a change in energetic flow? Because emotions are energy, and energy is a thing when in physical, rather than in spirit.

When emotions are experienced, or experiences are created, there is always a reason, a lesson to be learned. Or a belief that this, whatever it is, is needed in some way.

In other words, we commanded it, consciously or un-consciously. Therefore, it is very important that we discover, then acknowledge, and preserve the lesson. That way we never need to re-learn it.

In order to 'cleanly create' it is necessary to fully appreciate the power of the mind over the body. A typical mind power experience is fire-walking. Walking bare foot over red-hot coals without burning the soles of the feet. It's really important to understand just how much power the mind has over our energy flow. Gently taming and calming the mind is the way to the purest of health.

Remember:

You are who you believe yourself to be.
You get back what you think you deserve.

Systems and Connection

As counsellors, therapists, or healers we assist people to understand that they are not victims in relationships. Indeed, they chose them for a purpose. It's about regaining one's personal power. This is an important aspect of good health. As already discussed, the ideal question to ask when struggling with a relationship, or with a whole family group, is "what is there to learn from this family/relationship?" When the answer comes, ask "have I learned that lesson?" When you have you will be able to move forward.

Systems Analogy

Commonly hospitals are organized in order that specific floors are dedicated to specific health issues. Yet the air throughout the hospital is the same air. It is not different just because the floors are labelled oncology, or surgical. All floors are part of a whole hospital. They cannot be separated out. The human is not separate; we are part of a 'Wholistic Organic System.' It is important that we accept that parts of the body can never operate in isolation. They are all included in the wholeness. What affects one aspect, affects all aspects. There is no separateness in the body within or without. There is no distinction whatsoever.

Multiple aspects of religion, science, health, or beliefs, collect together then codify in a singular way. Indeed, a 'thought form' is created. We must understand how right the ancients really were in their concept of connectedness between all that exists. To further explain here is another analogy....

I bake Sour Dough bread. I need flour, water, salt, leaven, time for the dough to rise and a hot oven to bake it in. If I exclude leavening, don't use enough flour, don't put it in a hot oven, or don't allow enough time for rising, then my loaf is inedible. All ingredients and processes are equally valuable.

People generally don't see systems. To stay with the baking analogy, you can see a human cake mix as: Christianity, the eggs. Judaism, the leavening. Buddhism, the flavoring. Hinduism, the salt. Islam, the heat. Sikhism, the baking tin. Zoroastrianism, the milk. Aborigine beliefs are the mixing spoon. Wiccan the oven. Each ingredient being vital to producing a delicious cake. Anything in discord will cause a problem. We must embrace each other. Realize how important each is to the creation of a healthy system.

We Are All the Same No Difference

Perceived separation is the battle humanity is fighting. It's not just about good or evil belief systems, it's not that simple. The problem is the 'us and them' mindset. The attitude being 'they' are different to us. This leads to the belief that 'they are not like us therefore we can kill them, or take from them, with impunity.' We know where this kind of thinking leads. Aggression. Invasion. War. Yes, I've said it before but that had to be worth repeating.

Commune-ism

The Guides said "greed as a pseudo religion creates separation." They continued with "extreme Socialism, Fascism or Communism on a state scale don't work because of the creation of a single Leadership role (Totalitarian top down ruler)." As already mentioned, Beehives work well as community or system. All members of the hive know what their role is within the whole system of the hive. No direction or permission required. Mass agreement implicit within the hive. Bees do not need to be told what to do or allocated a job. They know instinctively how they must serve the whole hive, for the highest good of the community living there.

Mass agreement is required for any system to exist. For example, the banking system only works because of a mass agreement to value simple paper 'promissory notes.'

Judgment of self or others must cease for humanity to become healthy. Separatist behaviors must end. Here we've focused on the connectedness within the family group, or personal relationships.

I will allow you to extrapolate the concept out into the wider world for yourself.

We can only be healthy for ourselves. We cannot be healthy for others. However, we can have good intent for others.

I cannot stress enough the concept that unless separatist behavior stops, we will exterminate ourselves as a species.

We have already discussed the Zen concept of the effect on the world one butterfly can have by flapping its wings. The correct original quote is "if one moves in one place, one disperses and changes all other things around you." This is a basic Universal Law of Physics.

Judgment

Inferences are always based on judgment. Judgment comes first. We say 'this is to this, as this is not to this.' The original judgment comes first. It's termed SET Theory in Algebra. We need x to be given a value at the outset if we are to solve for x.

Wholeness

Personal health is achieved as a result of addressing perceived separate pieces, or parts of ourselves, then connecting them all back into the wholeness of us. Universal health is achieved by acknowledging the interaction between an individual human, humanity as community along with the universe as a whole. How we all interact with each other, or with the Earth, creates planetary level health.

Dr. Brené Brown PhD,[2] is a research professor at the University of Houston Graduate College of Social Work. She has spent the past thirteen years studying vulnerability, courage, worthiness, and shame. After years of research she has said, "Shame and fear are the un-ravellers of connection. Connection gives purpose and meaning to our lives. Connection is why we are here."

Dr. Brown has also said, "we must believe we are worthy of love and belonging in order to experience and attract love and belonging from others and the group."

Taking Responsibility

When we blame others, for what we should be responsible for, we do it to discharge pain or discomfort in ourselves. It is inappropriate to send that pain to others. Or to never release it from ourselves. Taking responsibility is key.

When we suppress or numb certain feelings, that we wish we did not have, we do not realize that by default, we are numbing all feelings. We are also suppressing our joy, hope, or happiness in addition to denying the pain. I once helped a client who said she had no childhood memories. After she had released the low vibrational emotions of anger, sadness, fear, hurt and guilt, she was delighted to report that suddenly she had begun to remember happy times from her childhood. Remember the unconscious mind will repress memories with unresolved emotional components to protect us.

Courage is the key to change. Courage has origins in the French language. It meant 'tell the story of who you really are from your heart.' The French word for heart is le cœur. If we are not courageous enough to allow ourselves to be seen or known as we truly are, without psychological masks or shields, then what hope do we have of healing or evolving?

Post Traumatic Stress Disorder (PTSD)

A new study has shown that Post Traumatic Stress Syndrome/Disorder, is not always rooted in the actual trauma of the experience. Often, after a trauma, the person is removed from others with whom they shared the experience. This separation then becomes a problem because of a lack of espirit de corps. All the others who had the shared experience are missing from everyday life.

There is a sense of being unable to relate to people who did not share the experience.

For example, soldiers who have strong camaraderie experienced as mutual trust and friendship, become connected through their hearts. Those same soldiers, when sent home on leave, may feel alone and unsafe as they are no longer part of a familiar group. The power of bonding together supports health. Retired military personnel often join specially sponsored groups to replace the camaraderie they felt in the armed services.

We are herd animals. We are not isolated loners. It is beneficial to connect through the heart when in a group, and then place intention that together the group can release the issues present in each member. This is simple because the discordant vibration of the issues becomes noticeable, and then with permission from each group member, can be released. There is power is in banding together. This is the basic foundation of the experience of contentment.

In cases of PTSD just helping the person to release the low vibrational emotions, then re-connecting them harically to Source and Earth, may not be enough. They may need to be connected through their heart to a group of other humans. For example, a self-help group, who have a strong espirit de corps. A group similar in nature to the group they were part of when the trauma occurred.

Any group that fills their need for tribe will be beneficial. We need to feel part of the herd. A functioning part of the Shtetl.³ We need to know where we fit into the puzzle, we call life. PTSD means individuals become disconnected from themselves and their world. They feel unsafe. Making it easier for the person to find the highest and best connection for themselves is the goal of the facilitator.

Modern day communes, or households comprising many single adults who get on together, can help each other regain health and wellbeing. The traditional 'Shtetl Community' had a very tribal way of living that supported the good health of its members. The people banded together, collectively farmed, and each person was seen to be of equal value.

As a child, Eddie Murphy was involved in a social program where inner-city kids were given holidays out in farming communities in order to learn how country folk lived. They were given a chance to experience the very opposite of what they had come to believe life was about in the inner-city environment. It was a very successful program. A win-win situation where farmers got help in their busiest season and the kids had their eyes opened to a bigger world-view.

In a group contagion assists the members who are not connected to Source and Earth to become connected. It is because vibration is contagious, that we can assist others regain flow, and create optimal vibration in themselves. Those who are connected enable others to connect, just like automatic role models. Contagion takes place due to the higher vibrations of those connected to Source and Earth. Good and bad spirits or moods are contagious.

It cannot be taken as read that if humans are connected through their SPP when in the presence of others, they will *always* be connected to Source and Earth. I like to avoid always, and never. I prefer to use frequent and rarely.

> At a symbolic level the Earth is our Mother. As a collective, humanity is raping her.
>
> - TOM KENYON

Here's a simple analogy. People know they need water and food yet, if they are unwell, they cannot obtain these basics for themselves. In which case others are happy to assist them. To take care of them. It's the same if someone is not connected to Source and Earth, yet someone in their group is connected. The 'connected one' can bring to the 'unconnected one' the connection they need. Intuitively people know what they need.

Humans cannot grow without connections to each other, and to Source and Earth. They can only survive not thrive.

The key to world peace is contagion of love and connectedness through community.

Remember the origin of evil is disconnection combined with lack of compassion.

There is only flow where energy is concerned. And how does it move? It flows towards love and therefore towards Source, or away from love, and therefore away from Source (which is towards the opposite polarity that we know as evil). A philanthropist[4] is a person who flows good out into others.

It bears repetition, the Guides have said many times, that unsustain-ability will result if the current destructive actions of humanity con-tinue. Full entropy will be the result. Many communities have de-stroyed themselves in the past.

Since we are so inter-connected, we will destroy ourselves and the Earth if we continue on our current trajectory without change.

The Energy of Conflict

When perceived psychically the energy of conflict looks like a knotted thread which tightens around those involved and also those who hear about the conflict. Be aware when speaking to others about issues, that you are winding them up with the thread and attaching them to you and the conflict. Would you like someone to do that to you?

Inner conflict within the self, is almost more debilitating that outer conflict with others. If there are parts or sub personalities battling against each other, a calm mind and homeostasis are hard to achieve.

Inner conflict caused by opposing belief systems is also damaging to health.

Review

- The understanding of how Insults affect system health is important
- Pivot Points are change points that are profound in their effect in a positive or negative way
- Find the antidote to the problem to cancel out the problem
- PTSD is now better understood in the context of systems
- Humans cannot grow without connections to each other, Source and Earth. They can only survive not thrive
- The key to world peace is contagion of love and connectedness through community
- Remember the origin of evil is disconnection combined with lack of compassion
- Take care when discussing areas of conflicts in your life as you are binding others to the issue

CHAPTER 5

FINDING WHO YOU REALLY ARE

The Hara Lines are the Seven Keys to
Health, Harmony, Success and Abundance.
-RITA MARR

THERE IS A SPECIFIC ASPECT of the energy system I call the Hara Dimension. The Hara Dimension is a meta program from which creation happens. Enormous creative power resides there. The energetic channels called the Hara Lines are the mainstay of our multidimensional connection to Eternal Source, to First Cause, and to the Earth. We all need to be connected in this way. Addressing the condition and connectivity of the hara lines is a good basic strategy that we all need to pay attention to. All mammals have the potential for this connection.

Hara Lines

Hara Lines are the source of our power, in other words our ability to have an effect on our world. When we tap into our inner power we are utilizing our Hara Lines. There are seven separate aspects to the Hara Line, which together comprise a main central channel (aka the Sushumna in Sanskrit).

I call the seven Hara Lines the Seven Keys to Health, Harmony, Success and Abundance.

Food is the source of fuel that we use to sustain us. Power has to be present first though, to support health.

We can repair and re-connect the hara lines to aid optimum and powerful energetic flow to aid health and healing.

The hara lines are pathways that allow energy to flow through the body. They are integral for health and life. If any of the hara lines are disconnected, we find ourselves feeling lost, afraid, and alone. Disconnection results in a victim mind-set because without the energy flowing in from Earth and Source, we allow ourselves to be manipulated from the outside. In situations of disconnection, we are not able to feel safe and trust our intuition, which comes from the 'heart mind.' In such a situation we often see the overwhelm of a person's will by the will of others.

Our journey is from victimhood to victor. Achieving our full unlimited potential together with strong fully functional hara lines are necessary in order to do that.

If the body's general vibration is low and yet the vibration in the hara lines is high, then we will be well health-wise. However, if the vibrations of both the body and the hara lines are low then dis-ease and/or ill-health will result. Many things bring down the vibration. For example, if the stomach and digestive system is vibrating at a lower rate due to toxic or poor-quality food, then the rest of the body's vibration will reduce to match the low vibration in the digestive system. Remember the movie *Supersize Me!?* An excellent example of this taking place.

Hara Lines help us perceive our world. They are constantly changing simply because our perception is in constant flux.

Hara Lines enable connection, perception, and interaction with the world. Therefore, they enable our ability to perceive differently at any given moment.

Lower vibrations (I have termed them 'insults') bring down the hara lines. Hara Lines are always there even if they are not optimally functional. Sometimes a hara line will be overworked and another underworked. Energy has to move, and if it cannot move in the designated way, just like water, it will find another route. Let's make the analogy of a road diversion if one route becomes impassable. Diversions onto other routes and roads enable traffic to flow, albeit less effectively. If energy becomes encumbered by a lower vibration it flows more slowly and sometimes less directly. Just like a diversion. Generally speaking, the lower the vibrations we are subjected to, the greater we will resist growth, evolution or the promptings of the intuition. I'm speaking in general terms; this is not a hard or fast truth. Good health is supported by fast freely flowing energy.

You could say that low vibrations are emotional storms rather than musical notes. Sounds that are very low some people find quite pleasing as they match the way they are feeling. However, these low sounds affect the physical being. Often, if we are feeling frustration or anger, and are unable to express the anger, we choose the low, thump, thump, of heavy metal type rock music to listen to. It resonates with our vibration. Birds of a feather flock together when it comes to vibrations. Sometimes base vibrations assist the body to release lower emotions.

As a general rule, rather than as a hard and fast rule, harp music can engender happy feelings due to the high vibrational notes. The high vibrational sounds of a piccolo may also engender happy feelings.

Tuning forks can assist in discounting the lower vibrations held within the human being. In this sense they act as a form of antidote or healing. If we are drawn to happier music when we are sad, we are intuitively using it as an antidote.

In Sedona USA, between 1981 and 1986, Camelback Hospital treated more than one hundred cocaine addicts a year, for the five-year period. A follow up survey carried out in 1986 showed that none of the patients who continued to listen to heavy metal rock music recovered.

The hara lines accurately reflect what our intention is at a core level in the moment of assessment. It's just impossible to fake this. We must

live our heart's promptings if we wish to be on purpose, not the promptings of our mind. Our heart and solar plexus provide reliable guidance.
The vibration of the hara should be higher than the vibration of the rest of
the body in order to support good health and well-being. The level of vibration of the individual, indicates their personal level of health.

Emotions are not Dictators

If we allow emotions to rule us, we need to learn that we can choose
otherwise. We are not our emotions. Even if we believe emotions are
our world that is clearly not the truth.

The color of the energy projected by the frequency of each of the seven
hara lines, other energetic pathways such as the meridians, and energy
centers such as chakras, dictate the health or otherwise of the body.

Reconnection

We reconnect our Hara Lines to cause health to occur. To create radiant health. Connection causes health.

The equation for good health is:

Correct abdominal Breathing
+ exercise
+ love to create connection
= health

We could say B+E+L+C = H

Seven Hara lines

There are five main hara lines, with one and seven consisting of two
lines, so the seven lines appear as five.

Multidimensional Connections

The hara lines are multidimensional and are designed to connect mammals, and humans, to the multi-dimensional nature of the Universe.

The Spirit selves (Higher Self, Soul, Monad) are not connected to third dimensionality in most people and this needs to be corrected.

Core Level Intentions

The hara lines accurately reflect what your intention is at a core level, in the moment the hara line is assessed. This intention cannot be faked. It's just like if you turn your head and look where you want to go, you also have to adjust the angle of your body to the same direction in order to successfully get there. Just turning the head and having the torso face another way, will mean you move in the direction the torso is facing, regardless of whether you are looking in that direction. You move in the direction your core is facing. If your core and your intention are at odds, then moving forward in the way you would like to, is compromised.

Hara Lines as Psychically Perceived

The hara lines are more easily psychically perceived by the observer in the area of the abdomen, at the hara center or below. It may be necessary to request that they become visible metaphysically. Their colors can be seen across the abdomen. They appear like the colored strings of a harp or thin ribbons of color. We can call them up by number and check their color, condition, and connectivity.

Figure 21 - Typical Maypole with its ribbons.

Maypoles Analogy

When we see the hara lines psychically, they do look like the colored lines of a 360-degree skirt, all around the body. Much like a Maypole with its ribbons.

The dance around the Maypole traditionally occurs May 1st each year. An old Pagan ceremony that has continued to this day in more orthodox religions. Often involving a young girl designated May Queen as the central attraction. It's certainly still a tradition in areas of England, France, Germany, Spain, Finland, Mexico, Canada, USA, and Jamaica. A ceremony that is said to honor the male and female and fecundity. Traditionally only girls would weave the ribbons around the very phallic like pole. It has crossed my mind that this could be representative of the colored hara lines being woven and un-woven around the central column some term the axis mundi, and my Guides call the balance connection. More ancient forgotten knowledge perhaps?

*Figure 22 – Traditionally only girls would weave the ribbons around the very phallic like pole which
I feel could represent the Main Central Channel of the Hara Lines.
Some poles have a tube torus shape at the top.*

Hara Line Colors

The individual hara lines are seen in their intrinsic colors (Figure 23). The main central channel is perceived as a greyish silver (a combination of all the hara colors). The colors are important because they are wavelengths. Color directs frequency. The eyes perceive color as wavelength. Each line's current status can be perceived as a 'shade' within the spectrum of the color. This is an indicator of the 'health or balance' in that hara line.

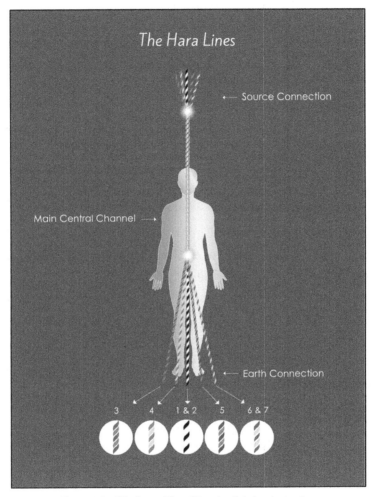

Figure 23 - The Seven Hara Lines in their intrinsic colors.

The higher the number of misperceptions and insults one has experienced, the more likely the line will be out of balance, which will reflect in its color and status.

In the healing scenario, putting intention on the change of color we require for our health and well-being, will bring about a shift which honors the persons highest good. This is an example of working with issues as energy to bring about mental, emotional, and physical change.

The Hara Center

The main Hara Lines one and two, the balance connection, are usually seen towards the center of the body. The minor lines three, four, five, six and seven are more easily seen psychically as they branch out and down, usually around the hara center. The branching area may be in a slightly different place in each person.

A simple visual would be to imagine the lines as colored multiple fine ribbons, filaments, or strings around a central point. The hara center is located close to the sacral area but behind it and deeper into the body. The hara center embraces the hara lines through 360°.

Hara Lines One and Two

Health originates in the center of the body through Hara Line One and Two which are colored black and white, respectively. These two lines are twisted together in a rope like way. The black and white represent the level of light and dark within us. Ideally, we need a balance of the two. Therefore, when seen with psychic sight, due to the nature of their spin, the two colors are blended and a silvery grey shade results. If these Hara Lines are flawed or compromised, then health issues result, either on a mental or physical level.

Line one and two have also been termed the 'balance connection' by my Guides. In the Hindu tradition Hara Line One is called the Ida Nadi and links to the moon and darkness. Hara Line Two is called the Pingali Nadi and links to the sun and lightness. The polarity of light and dark is present here and is reflected as hope and despair. Too much darkness will be revealed as depression or an inability to contribute. Too much lightness as flightiness. It's important to realize that we can equalize the dark and the light.

Hara Line one connects us to 'Now'. The breath is the driver of now-ness. Hara Line two connects us to non-egoic 'Will,' also known as Intention.

Figure 24 - Hara lines one and two are termed 'the balance connection.'

Our entire life progression is contained here as one moment.

Disconnection or lack of highest and best function in hara lines one and two affects personal power levels. Lines one and two are in essence an energetic gyroscope. People with strong 'presence' have lines one and two strongly connected. Flighty 'will o'the wisp' types lack connectivity through lines one and two to some degree. To move from a lack of presence to presence we must ensure one and two are fully connected and functioning at highest and best.

Hara Line Three

Hara Line Three's ideal color is deep forest green. Line three is called 'Navigation' or the 'Tribal' line. In other words, it represents the 'Essence' of each of us and how we relate with others of our tribe, group or nation. This energy will be picked up by others who will sense if we are from their tribe, or in some way like them.

We sense the others who vibrate as we do, in other words those who share our tribal ancestral line. This line is not affected by adoption. Adopted children will always feel the connection with their birth parents if they were ever to meet them.

Sally and I sensed the third hara line vibration when we first met. We felt it before we discussed what was causing the resonance. We may have distant ancestors in common as we both hail from the Celtic gene pool.

Figure 25 - Hara line three, Navigation, I term the Lighthouse,
as it keeps us on course in safe waters.

Hara Line three reflects whether we are accident prone either physically or emotionally. This is because a lack of grounded-ness through this line often reflects in accidents. The grounding offered by this line is much stronger than through the base chakra or feet. It's also a navigational beacon. How comfortable we are with breathing is reflected here. As is a sense of belonging, safety, and security. Other teachers in the past may have simply referred to this line as grounding but this channel is much more than that.

I call Hara Line three The Lighthouse as it keeps us on course in the safe waters.

Receiving may be limited and resisted by self-sacrifice through this line. Nervous system insults that affect this line at a young age cause autism. Insults bend, misalign or disconnect lines. Insults through this line affect immune system function.

Hara Line Four

Hara Line Four is the 'Receiving' line. It helps us receive gracefully.

It's closely linked to the physical plane and physical body. The color comprises shades of yellow to vermilion red. This line is all about receiving, from basic sustenance like food and drink, to taking in health and allowing the Earth to sustain us while we live on her body. The theme of this line is nurturance, acceptance, how the body receives good things. How we process compliments. Auto immune disorder manifests when this line is out of calibration. Which in effect means that the person has an unconscious desire to give up on life.

Figure 26 - Hara Line Four enables us to receive abundance.

Shifting color denotes how well we are receiving. Lighter towards yellow means less able to receive, less able to allow in goodness. Darker towards vermillion means more willing to receive, or allow goodness in.

An overload of industrial chemicals and toxins in the air or water, or heavy metal adjuvants in vaccines, result in insults which in turn create physical health issues through this line. Along with line three, Autism can be related to lack of function in this line.

A richer color denotes being more open to receive. In auto immune disease the line will be pale yellow to almost no yellow.

This line can become truncated if we perceive we are receiving too much.

Rules such as "should not" and "have to" truncate hara line four.

Hara Line Five

Hara Line five is the 'Life Purpose' channel. Its focus is spiritual growth. Alignment with Eternal Source as First Cause. Hara Line Five keeps us 'on purpose.'

Its color is shades of blue to indigo. It's our life force. It's purposefulness. This line's theme is owning one's progress. The Dalai Lama for example will have a strong line. Here it is not a consideration of health, but a consideration of connection. A pale blue line will reflect an attitude of 'I don't know why I'm here.' A dark indigo will reflect an attitude of 'I know my purpose and I'm striving for it. I'm getting to know where I fit into the grand scheme of the Synocratic system that is humanity on the Earth. I'm understanding who I am in the context of others.' This is the least important line in the third dimension. It's very important in the second, fourth, fifth, and sixth dimension. Overly identifying with one's job or position in career rather than our authenticity of being is reflected here.

Figure 27 - Hara Line Five is the life purpose channel.

Obsession can be an indicator of an out of balance hara line five.

Pedophilia shows itself here as a learned behavior due to childhood sexual abuse. Pedophiles are not born to be that way, they are trained by their abusers.

If you are born to achieve a certain purpose, and you do so, then Hara Line three Green (Navigation and Tribe) shows that. If you *become* your intent, then line five (Life Purpose) shows that.

Criminals may become criminally minded and feel at ease with criminal activity due to influence, conditioning, or choices. That being the case hara line five will reflect that choice rather than hara line three, which would show if they were born to that way of life.

You are not a pawn—you are the engineer and architect of your life. You may choose to stop being buffeted by the world. You can take back your power. You can restore that which you perceive has been ruined and make it more beautiful than before.

Hara Lines Six and Seven

Hara Lines six and seven are the sexuality lines, incorporating resilience, and strength and energy.

They are twisted together and may appear as one line shaded red to pink. Line six, pink, is feminine gender and line seven, red, is masculine gender. The shades reflect different 'temperatures' of the same color. Hara Line six is related to resilience in a person. It is possible to build resilience by ensuring line six is functioning optimally. Hara Line seven is related to strength and energy.

Figure 28 - Hara Lines Six and Seven are male and female sexuality lines.

These sexuality lines are open to alteration by the free will of the individual. Heterosexuality, homosexuality, and bisexuality are free will choices. These lines are also influenced by trauma or insults in this life or past lives. A person can choose which sexual preference they wish to affiliate with, and whether they wish to pro-create.

Line six and seven is a natural population controller which may be adjusted biochemically whilst the baby is in the womb. In other words, line six and seven dictate the birth sex of the baby due to three main influences:

1. Pressure on the planet regarding numbers of population
2. Personal trauma or insults from past lives
3. Emotional support issues. For example, a belief by a female that males as partners are unsupportive, means she will choose same sex lesbian relationships instead

Homosexuality is therefore reflected in these lines. Homosexuality is a free will choice made because of past life experiences, humanity's natural population control, or personal beliefs. A homosexual male's line will be closer to pink. A homosexual female's line will be closer to red.

It's worth repeating here that Pedophilia is a taught and learned behavior. Abuse is the teacher and it infects generation after generation as I have already said. Trauma is involved which results in insults. This type of experience links to Life Purpose line five not to sexuality lines six or seven.

Healing Through the Hara Lines
In the healing scenario putting intention on the change of color we require for our health and well-being will bring about a shift which honors the persons highest good. This is an example of working with energy to bring about mental, emotional and physical change.

Remember that the hara lines are multidimensional and are designed to connect people to the multi-dimensional nature of the Universe.

Trauma and the Hara Lines
Trauma, (I prefer the term insult), detrimentally affects the functioning of the Hara Lines. The insults may be physical, for example a physical blow, accident, or toxin. Or emotional. For example, emotional blackmail by others, or self-inflicted self-sabotage.

The hara lines may be termed 'set' when they are functioning and correctly calibrated. Unset when they are out of calibration.

The majority of people are born with all the Hara Lines in calibration. Occasionally one or two may be un-calibrated, or turned off by choice, in order to fulfil a purpose, or due to karmic experience. If this is the case, we must be careful never to force a re-connection.

The hara lines are the beginning of plugging into the planet. However, it goes far beyond that. The lines also enable the unplugging of multiple selves. Together with clearing in the Universe.

The Quantum and the Newtonian (mechanical) world view together create conflict and therefore cause imbalance. This is why I have gone to great lengths to explain the truth of how our reality is created and how it functions.

I work in quantum entanglement with clients, this is the only way I can connect successfully and effect change. I use the many worlds and multiple selves' theory and attractive sympathetic vibration.

Hara Lines in Relation to the Other Energetic Aspects

The Merkeba[1] relies on the Hara Lines as an anchor. A healthy functional Merkeba is crucial for health and ascension.

Sometimes the priority for healing is not at the haric level. In which case, of course, we would attend to the priority which needed be healed first. This may be chakra's, meridians, subtle body or auric field levels.

Let's take the analogy of a house. The hara lines are the structure of the building. Other energetic aspects are like the furniture and furnishings.

The hara lines are one piece of the puzzle that is the human energy system. Picture a large book, an enormous tome, that is representative of the entire human energy system. Only one sixth of the pages would contain information pertaining to the hara lines.

That being said, when the structure of the house is poor, the house is unsound and could topple. If a wise craftsman was called in to remedy the problem and he does his job well, he knows what to remedy first and the right order of priority for the other jobs. The hara lines comprise only one sixth of the human energy system. When the structure is poor and unsound however, the house falls down!

Each Line Has a Color

The colors are important because they are wavelengths. The eyes perceive color as wave-lengths. Each line's current status can be perceived as a 'shade' within the spectrum of the color. This is an indicator of the 'health or balance' in that hara line. The higher the number of misperceptions or insults the more likely the line to be out of balance, or the wrong color.

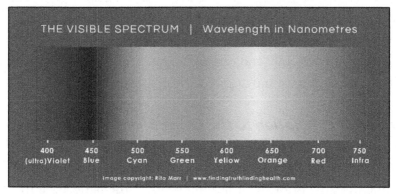

Figure 29 - The Hara Line Colors are indicative of different wavelengths.

We ourselves can intend the color to change by using visualization. Simply visualizing oneself coloring the line with metaphysical paint will affect the line's frequency. Or by simply looking at a color wheel, choosing the color the line is now, and another shade to represent what we want it to become, then putting our intention on changing it, will bring about the shift which honors the highest good.

The Importance of the Facilitator's Pure Intention

Pure potential enables the optimal placement in that moment of time for that individual. Remember that the Higher Self does the directing, the facilitator's job is simply to unlock. The Higher self finds the highest and best state to suit the human at the time. Respect from Practitioner for client is key.

A real-life example of hara line healing:

Tanya experienced painful sinus infections every six months which also caused pain in the bottom jaw and she came to me because her strong painkillers had induced vomiting for a whole day. Her body was rejecting food and medication.

I found Hara line four was truncated and there was fear of receiving. Tanya only reluctantly allowed herself to receive, because there was the expectation that the giver will expect something in return that she cannot provide or give. There was fear of being unable to fulfil the expectations of others who have given to her (particularly her mother). Tanya's unconscious conclusion was 'it's better to not receive.' I unblocked three points, two in the solar plexus area and one in the sacral area and repaired hara line four.

Hara Line Five was also truncated due to insults received between ages five to ten so we assisted her inner child to heal its wounds and repaired Hara Line Five.

Tanya works with color and energy on a daily basis as an intuitive healer. In her own words she reported "the first immediate and obvious change during the therapy sessions I have with Rita is the vibrancy in the colors I perceive, and the way in which they affect my subtle bodies for the better. The relief from the sinus pain was almost immediate. My physical body responded with such relief that the swelling and tiny bit of residual pain dissipated over a matter of hours."

Two weeks later Tanya reported that she feels she can now receive with gracefulness and gratitude and had also realized that it is safe to express her own feelings when hurting.

Again, in her own words "the peace I have in my entire body is one I have never felt before. I am beginning to realize how that old pain and hurt that I was holding onto made it difficult to move forward. I am in awe of my body's healing ability."

Animal Hara Lines

In domestic four-legged animals the process of haric alignment is similar to the process I would use for their human owner.

Wild non-domesticated animals differ in hara design.

Pet Birds are like shapeshifters, in that some can have the same arrangement and alignment as their human owner, others may be different.

Dog and Cat Hara Line Location

In dogs and cats Hara Line one and two enter through the crown of the head and leave through the navel area into the Earth. The other hara lines can be perceived near the navel area.

When stepping into the field of a four-legged animal to offer healing it is best to approach them mid abdomen, near the final rib, as this is their balance point. Avoid looking into their eyes.

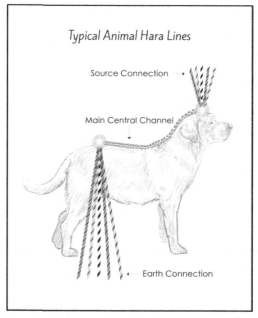

Figure 30 - In dogs Hara Line One and Two enter through the crown of the head and leave through the navel area into the Earth.

Symptoms of Haric Disconnection

The majority of people these days are not happy, but they don't know why, or even what it would take to make them happy. The Council of Truth say over 45% of the population are in need of energetic repair work to enable them to function at highest and best. In many cases re-connection and energetic repair on various levels will enable us to fully connect to our whole-selves.

The Soul is a unitive beautiful extension of our physical being which is connected to everyone and everything. When we are disconnected from the unity of humanity, we feel uncomfortable, or bereft, but we often don't consciously know what is causing us to feel that way. We cannot discover who we really are, why we are here, where we need to go, and for what purpose, if we are not connected to Source and Earth.

We are not able to feel fulfilled until we realize that we are one tiny cog in the engine wheels of Unity and we have our own unique part to play. A feeling of happiness, motivation, achievement, and fulfilment is the natural outcome of being connected and successfully playing our part in the 'beehive of humanity.'

I often ask people the following questions:

- Are you fulfilled in life?
- Are you attracting the abundance you deserve?
- Do you feel you know why you are here? Your purpose?
- Are you happy with your level of emotional, mental, physical and spiritual health?

A 'no' answer to any of these indicates lack of haric alignment.

Here are some typical issues which are commonly addressed through haric alignment.

- Loss of grounding
- Loss of Inner strength
- Loss of an Inner sense of security
- Identity Crisis, or inner conflict around identity
- Feeling abandoned, alone, vulnerable
- Feeling you are under psychic attack
- Survival issues
- Anxiety or panic attacks

- Difficulty in receiving or accepting good things
- Using the Head Mind and Heart Mind separately rather than together
- Feeling Lost and Alone
- Unable to move forward
- Feeling stuck
- Lacking direction in life
- Lost connection with your purpose
- Lack inspiration or drive
- Frustration at lack of achievement or success
- Inability to cope with life in general
- Living in chaos

In the case of haric disconnection, people find themselves feeling lost, afraid, and alone. Disconnection results in a victim mindset. It allows us to be manipulated from the outside. In situations of disconnection, we are not able to feel safe and trust intuition of the heart. This is where we see the overwhelm of the will of one person by the will of others.

Reconnection Causes Health and Evolution

If the Spirit Selves are not fully connected to the physical being in third dimensionality in over 45% of the population, my strong feeling is that this needs to be corrected if we are to evolve as a race.

Our connection to the Multi-dimensional nature of the Universe causes health to occur, therefore, after the re-connection of our hara lines a return to health is supported. Yes, it's true that re-connection causes health.

The higher the number of emotional or physical 'insults' i.e. misperceptions, the more likely a line will be out of balance and in need of repair.

Lines of Contagion and Connection

All living things have horizontal lines emanating from them into the space around them. These lines enable contagion, a phenomenon we discussed earlier when we discussed connectedness. These lines enable all living things to connect. It is through these lines of contagion that we sense the intentions of others by sampling their energetic precedence (this is more than the aura as commonly defined). The horizontal lines of contagion connection enable energetic readings to be detected by other living things. All mammals have this energy flow. These horizontal lines are multiple and varied and in fact radiate outwards from the center of the being (usually from solar plexus and heart area).

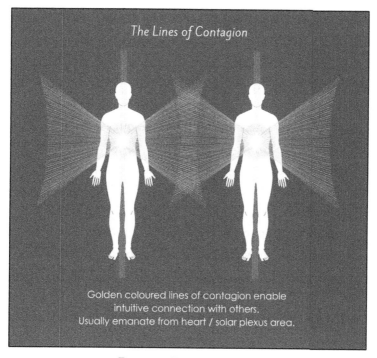

Figure 31 - Lines of Contagion.

The Lines of Contagion, that function purely to connect us with others and the world around us, were known and understood in the ancient Huna teachings and were termed by them 'aka cords'.

If we were to see the energy lines of a human on the level of contagion, we would notice a cross like structure with a vertical movement of energy from above the head to below the toes. In addition, energy moves horizontally, across and through us in a 'wing like' way. This flow of energy applies to all living things.

The Hara Lines are aspects of our connection to the Earth and Source. Whereas the horizontal emanations, the lines of contagion, because they are receiving information from outside, from others and the environment, could be considered more of a non-personal line or an interactive line. Describing more about the nature of the horizontal lines of contagion is beyond the scope of this book.

Dark Matter, aka Anti-matter, in the Context of Healing

It is important that we understand there are different facets of energy. Dark matter is one such facet. Dark matter as we have discussed is the other side of the mirror as it were. Imagine the Earth together with humanity, are on one side of a mirror, and there is another side, let's term it the dark side. Therefore, if we place our issues, misperceptions, misapprehensions and imagined limitations, or inhibitions, into dark matter, with or without conscious intention, change occurs, and resolution happens. Also, if we are not doing well it may be that we need to bring forth from dark matter the missing pieces that contribute to our individual wholeness once again. Bits and pieces of energy can find their way to dark matter without our conscious awareness. Having explained that, I want to stress that I would never recommend sending issues into dark matter deliberately. Better to release them and transmute them back into Light from whence they came.

Correspondingly the Earth and humanity represents the dark side to 'others.' This is why hara line number one and two are black and white.

Different facets of energy are the natural state, and it's how energy moves in all universes at all times. The only difference in a Universal sense is the chemical make-up of the stars, and physicality, of a particular Universe. The same rules and laws apply everywhere. The analogy would be of pots of different colored paint. Each pot is the same in its viscosity, its adhesion abilities, and its drying time, yet each pot may be perceived differently purely on the basis of its color. The only difference is the way the light reflects from each 'color' in a specific place in a Universe.

Balance the Light and Dark Within

Hara Line One and Two are representative of Light and Dark. Optimal balance in these lines is the goal for each and every person. Everyone should aspire to that optimal balance. Yet this act of balancing the light and the dark is filled with folklore, spiritual traditions and dressed up with metaphor and story. Getting the balance of light and dark within us is like balancing on a ball. We must avoid falling into one-sidedness. People who are 'flighty' and not connected to the Earth, in other words are all light with no darkness, are not in a position to contribute to humanity because they are not grounded. Similarly, people with too much darkness are not able to contribute either because they will feel 'depressed' or down. This is not a judgment. We avoid judgments!

Evil is not to be judged in terms only of light or dark. Darkness is just a vibration, a dark color designation. Lightness is a vibration designated white on the spectrum. Both black and white contain all the colors. White light contains all colors of light as evidenced by a prism. Black emerges if red, yellow and blue paint are combined.

The Energetic Precedence

There is an extension of the human body that moves before us which my Guides call the Energetic Precedence. This is larger and much more complex than what we commonly term the Aura. It is through the Energetic Precedence that people connect and sense instant rapport, like, attraction, instant rejection or dislike. Whether they feel safe or unsafe around a certain individual. This is intrinsic. In other words, inherent, innate, natural, and built-in. It's a protection mechanism. Cultivated from early mammals who have it too. It's an ability to read the 'Essence of the other.' Primates do it naturally and in consequence do it very well.

In July 1960, at the age of twenty-six, Jane Goodall travelled from England to what is now Tanzania in Africa, and bravely entered the little-known world of wild chimpanzees. Armed with nothing more than her notebook and a pair of binoculars she used her patience and continued optimism to gain the trust of these initially shy creatures. She was able to allow us a peak into the world of primates which seems, conflictingly, familiar, and yet strange. Watching her videos[2] you will see the phenomena of chimpanzees reading one another through the energetic precedence very clearly. It's fascinating.

The energetic precedence allows us to 'absorb', and sample, the energy of the other, and in doing so instantly 'know' if we are safe around this person or not. What are we reading? Is it the color, the vibration, or intention? The essence or mood of the Energetic Precedence? This energy field, which goes ahead of each person, broadcasts who, and what, we are. We can quite naturally and easily sample the Essence of the person as they move through time and space. It is either unwelcoming or welcoming. It is this 'temperature' within the energetic precedence that signals to the other person connection, health, and intent. We know if we are meeting a person who is of our tribe. Whether they are well, sick and what their intention is. All humans can use this natural ability to sense, and know, via the means of the energetic precedence. However, most have forgotten how to do it.

How do we innately do this? Well, everyone has experienced the energetic precedence feeding back to them when they view a prospective house to buy or rent. We know almost immediately we walk over the threshold if we could live there. This happens independently of what we see around us in the rooms. We also know if we are attracted or repelled when meeting someone for the first time.

Energy Is the Source of Change, Growth or Stagnation

A short study of Ayurvedic or Chinese medicine is a great way to understand the concept of energy channels projecting in order that others may perceive our nature and essence.

We are energy. Electrical energy first and foremost. Our Physical nature is formed second. As our energy is, so we become. Energy is the source of change, growth, or stagnation.

The Contagion of Energy

All energy is contagious whether its light or dark, high vibration, or low. All humans know the trick of hanging out with successful people if you wish to be successful. Personal development, and Neuro Linguistic Programming Coaches and Trainers capitalized on the concept of growth being contagious. I will endeavor here to connect the pieces together.

We now know that it is within our Energetic Precedence (EP) where we gather information or learn lessons about the other and that this was originally designed purely as a survival tactic. All mammals and some non-mammals have this ability. Birds utilize this. Small birds will be careful around larger predatory birds. Members of the flock know whether a bird is part of their flock and they also know if the other bird is healthy. Females can choose the strongest, healthiest, best gene pool when selecting a mate, using the same ability.

I rarely watch TV. However, years ago I watched a UK TV show called *Long Lost Family*. The featured mother said, when she met her daughter for the first time since she was taken for adoption as a baby forty-one years earlier: "I feel like an animal that's recognized its young. My heart just went out and I knew she was mine. The maternal feeling just came out. It felt like she was mine the moment I touched her. I felt an immediate bond when we hugged."

Have you ever wondered how it is that when someone yawns you also spontaneously yawn? How when someone has tears of joy you do also. When someone on stage performs a particularly emotive song the whole audience feels the same emotion and reacts? This is the horizontal lines of contagion/connection in action. This input of information is happening every waking moment, sometimes consciously and sometimes not.

Social Media enables contagion and entanglement without being in the same room. Movies and TV enable contagion too. This is why discernment and selectiveness is necessary if you wish to remain clear of infection by the low vibrations generated by others, deliberately or otherwise.

In the past we have been losing our ability to read others through the

Energetic Precedence because these days we tend to rely on our heads and rational thought. To listen to the messages being passed through the EP we must use our intuition, our gut feel, our heart mind. More on the heart mind later. Some people even build a type of energetic 'wall' at the shoulders and refuse to go below that. Literally this creates a 'talking head'. Just throat and head. Look at media talking heads. We look at the outside and who's doing the talking, rather than rely on the EP's transmission which is like a satellite receiver of information we can decode.

Connection

There is a giant need for connection in humanity these days because of a lack of tribal community. Essentially if a person is lonely, tribe-less, or feels emotionally isolated, this can be a source of disease [dis-ease where we are 'ill at ease' which is defined as uncomfortable, embarrassed, uneasy, self-conscious, out of place, inhibited, gauche]. We affect change in ourselves at the level of the contagious nature of who we choose to be.

Contagion and Entrainment

In groups energy is contagious. Fact. A phenomenon known as entrainment is always at work between people. If entrainment enables a low vibration to increase to a higher vibration, then the person who had the lower vibration benefits. If the opposite happens then the one whose vibration is lowered by the other suffers. In chemistry, when the differing Ph. level of two fluids, each on the opposite sides of an osmotic membrane, are placed together, the lower ph. level will increase to match the higher ph. level and the two will end up equal. This is not always the case with humans however. Sometimes those people with a lower vibration can win and bring all those around them down to their low level. The mind often drags us down into a lower vibration by causing states of worry, fear, anxiety, or frustration. We can offset this by moving into our SPP and out of our heads.

How to access the SPP is taught in my live Webinars and mentioned later in this book. Living life from the SPP leads us into fortitude, courage and high vibrationary states. We can only evolve and ascend when we access and use the SPP.

The Layers of Man & Healing the Energetic Precedence

The following information is not new but it is certainly worthy of repeating.

Through altruism we can assist and help one another. Put simply a small kindness can cause a change in the way the energy flows in another person for the better. Shakespeare[3] put it so eloquently (see quote).

> The quality of mercy is not strained.
> It droppeth as the gentle rain from heaven upon the place beneath.
> It is twice blessed: it blesseth him that gives and him that takes.
>
> – SHAKESPEARE

On the other hand, a slight, an insult, a rejection, a snub, disrespect, a rebuff, disregard, ignoring or scorning another can do harm.

The movie *Paying It Forward* is a good example of small kindnesses being harbingers of change and healing. Smiles and laughter are contagious. Just as depression and fear are contagious. The unfortunate truth is though, that bad things are usually more interesting to people. Hence the news media focus on the problems of the world. A Soul's vibrational level dictates what they are interested in. They can only attract a similar vibration. Therefore, good vibes attract good. The opposite is also true because like attracts like. But it's all just energy really.

Judgment v Factual Assessment

Judgment on what is positive or negative is inappropriate. What is appropriate however is to assess what is beneficial, or not beneficial, to us. What is advantageous or detrimental from a growth or connection point of view. This is factual assessment and therefore not judgment.

It is how we apply judgment to our (often erroneous) perceptions that cause our own issues.

Energetic Precedence Layers

The Inner field which lies up to eighteen inches (46 cms) out from the physical body within the close EP is where we 'feel.' Where we interpret the information, or emotions of others, we are sensing through our lines of contagion, and the area where we feel our own emotions. This inner field is called the Astral Body. The Astral Body encompasses both the emotional and mental subtle bodies. This is where we hold, or release by clearing, emotions and limiting beliefs. Toxins, stuckness and stagnancy create lack of flow in the emotional body. All health, and all disease, begins outside the physical body within the Astral Body. Emotional storms take place in the Astral. This being the case how does one affect change at the astral level?

Affecting Change at an Astral Level

There are four ways and only the first two are default methods. The second two are learned during our evolution and these are the preferred ways to release emotions to effect better health.

a) **Dispersal**

Most common. The easiest.

This is where we off-load onto the nearest person. When we experience emotional storms, we want to exit them as soon as possible, and most people know no other way than by off-loading them onto others.

For example, a depressed person will feel better after a happy visitor leaves. The formerly happy visitor may feel depressed or drained however, after being in the company of the depressive. The feeling of being drained by another person is a common experience. Most of us will experience it at some point in our lives. Road rage is an example of another form of discharge. Sometimes young children or babies discharge through their mother because they cannot physically do it for themselves. Years ago, I was giving an energy healing to a small baby at the request of its mother. Mom, who was sitting quietly in the room, suddenly jumped up, ran to the bathroom, and vomited. When she returned I asked her how she had felt just before the nausea.

She said she was fine. There was no prior indication of the need to vomit. I realized that the child had needed to release and could not do so itself. The mother was consciously unaware that she had volunteered to process the release in a way that the baby could not.

b) **Breathing** (Conscious or deep)

This is much healthier way than (a) Dispersal, because it enables emotional storms to move through. Emotional storms can only happen during a holding of the breath. Marathon Runners often clear their emotions in this way. It's a good coping mechanism for them and explains why they get anxious when they are not running regularly. They disperse through the breath. It's not the exercise, it's just the breath.

c) **Haric Alignment**

Through a connection to Source and Earth via the Hara Lines. This is a healthier way by far than a) and b). More about this later.

d) **Understanding** (highest way)

Understand the messages and learnings being offered by the e-motion (energy in motion).

The messages are important and offer us important opportunities to learn the lessons we came here to learn. We must learn, then release the emotion. This is a universal message given by many religions and spiritual teachings. We will re-visit this concept in the context of spiritual growth and how one achieves enlightenment. Basically, enlightenment is getting over yourself!! Easy to say, difficult to do.

Energetic Flow Within the Physical Body Promotes Health

Let us review what we have learned thus far about who we are energetically. We have many layers to our being. Let us term them the Layers of Man.

The Layers of Man

1. A framework of energy - the energetic precedence and energy channels of the body
2. A layer of unconscious thought over the energy framework
3. Conscious thought on top of that
4. The information from the lines of Contagion going in and out, on top of that
5. Exterior connection to Source above and Earth below through the Hara Lines

Most people are cognoscente only of layer four. They are aware only of the information going in and out. They have no clue about the other layers, their existence or function. The purpose here is to expand your knowing and understanding of all the other Layers. We need to be in balance at all five levels in order to support good health.

Haric Alignment and Healing

I always start by assessing the main hara lines one then two. I ask my Higher Self in turn, "Has this hara line become unset?"

Then I ask the person to reply verbally to the question: "Do you wish to be re-connected to multi dimensionality?"

Then I ask my Higher Self "in what way will the highest and best function be restored to this hara line?"

The healing of each Hara Line involves removing any unsetting, occlusion, truncation, over extension, misalignment, or disconnection, from the earth's core or from Source.

The lines themselves should not be seen as one single strand but many strands like a fiber optic cable. Ideally the energy needs to flow through all strands.

When it comes to energy flow it's just like when the road is closed and one takes the diversion. There are many roads that lead to the same location in a city. If one way is congested simply choose another. Such is the truth of human healing.

By asking, "In what way will the highest and best function of this hara line be restored?" healing can be initiated.

There are many reasons why there are disconnections from Source and Earth. My intention is to bring healing to enable a return to balance so all becomes possible. Sometimes additional emotional clearing is required to assist healing on a physical level. Often an attitude of yielding or surrendering is necessary in the client. Sometimes one needs to accept one's innate state as perfection for you.

Feelings are only information. Emotions are not meant to control humans. Humans are meant to remain in control as information is presented to them. Welcome the information in order that it ceases to have power over you. Messages that are always useful to us if we will but take notice of them. I'm sure you have noticed that when a small child wishes to attract the attention of an adult the strategy usually consists of continual poking, or pulling at clothes, until the adult takes notice of them. This plays out in life if we continually refuse to take notice of our emotional messages.

Picking up the vibration of others can either raise or lower your own vibration as already mentioned.

Perceived insults, or discordant traumas, whether emotional (betrayal), or physical (as in a blow) affect the function and calibration of all hara lines. This is termed 'Unsetting.'

If the general body vibration is low and yet the vibration in the hara lines is high, then the person will be well and healthy. However, if the vibrations of both the body and the hara lines are low then dis-ease or poor health will result.

Many things bring down the vibration. For example, if the stomach and digestive system is vibrating at a lower rate due to toxic food it will bring the rest of the body down to the same vibration. Just like when you toss a pebble into a pool of water. A wave is caused. Then more and more waves move outward until the waves touch and counteract each other.

What If?

When we consider our 'health' we must consider our wholeness. Focusing only on one small part rarely works. It's not just about individual hara lines but how they interact with all other lines, the Earth, and Source, from where the power comes. Then of course there are the vibrations in our community or family that 'infect' us because they are contagious. Every aspect of healing must always be connected back to the wholeness. The effect of an interaction between one individual and the rest of humanity, or with the universe as a whole, must be acknowledged.

Remember the effect one butterfly can have by flapping its wings. How we all interact with each other and with the Earth creates health.

We all need to do our bit. Re-connect your hara lines and in doing so raise your vibration. Eventually the tipping point will be reached and we will all be living as our fully conscious selves and Mother Earth will be supported as she heals herself.

How We Stop Ourselves Receiving

If it's true that abundance is our natural state, then why do many of us feel unable to tap into the consciousness of abundance? Well, if we are optimally connected to Source and Earth then we have a better chance of attracting abundance. There are many reasons why we become disconnected from Source and Earth.

As I've already covered, traumas (insults or mis-perceptions) whether physical or emotional, can affect the function and calibration of all energetic flows within us, including those of our Hara Lines which are our main energetic connection to Source and Earth.

The energy of intentionality is accessed through Hara Line Two. If Hara Line Two is not functioning then you cannot use your will to create what you want. There are other reasons creation is inhibited. For example, If Hara Line Four (Receiving), is truncated, it has the same effect as omitting to pull out the antenna of a radio. Reception (receiving) will be weak. Other reasons receiving can be inhibited involve Hara Line Five, or Three or both.

If one holds extreme views on a subject Hara Line Five (Life Purpose) can affect receiving due to the need to resist or reject. These attitudes will act as filters which stop or inhibit receiving. Hara Line Three, if operating under the attitude of self-sacrifice as an extreme view, (I'm here to be a soccer ball instead of a human), will also inhibit receiving.

People who are in this position need to be treated gently, softly and compassionately. The best approach is to give them space and opportunity to approach the facilitator. Let them come to you. They must not feel threatened because entrenched beliefs are easily threatened by a new concept. It is best to use grand generalities. Vagueness before specifics. If/then presuppositions, for example, '*If* you choose to be different *then* you can.' Or *if* you agree to change *then* that means change can occur easily. Metaphors that switch focus to a third party also displace resistance and may be used to great effect. A lot of people understand that animals respond best if not cajoled or threatened. We are the same in that respect.

Remember that the hara lines accurately reflect what your intention is at a core level in the moment the hara line is assessed. This intention cannot be faked.

Success Story

Let me share the story of a woman who had suffered from constipation for over twenty years, and who also experienced constant feelings of being inert, overwhelmed and stuck. Hara lines indicate health or illness through their color. Each line is designed to have a wavelength that is perceived as a specific color.

On inspection her Hara Line Three was an inappropriate color. Instead of deep forest green it was a turquoise pale green shade. Plus, Hara Line Five was an inappropriate red color, instead of blue. What was there to learn from this phenomenon? The client felt that for years she had been at odds with how she was conditioned to behave. In other words, she was no longer able to fully act according to her entrenched belief "women should behave well all the time and never express their feelings." It was apparent that the woman had subjugated her will to others, in the hope that they would like her. This had taken place at around age eleven. Her life lesson could have been to overcome allowing the will of others to dominate her own. The healing was placed in the client's field so she could take it if she chose to. It was likely if nothing changed that a major health problem would manifest in the colon area. The insults had been continuing from age eleven. It was not just one event but many events over forty years. This compounded the problem. The hara lines reflected complete changes from their designated colors. The good news is that this lady chose to heal. Her hara line colors adjusted to reflect her choice.

It can be a 'chicken and egg' situation sometimes when working at the haric level. If we change the colors consciously, and we are ready to yield to healing, then we positively affect the health. If we choose to accept a healing intervention, then the colors automatically change to reflect that choice.

The Hara Center and Tan Tien

The Hara Center is located five centimeters (two and a half inches) below the navel. It has the appearance of a sphere one and a half inches (3.81 centimeters) in diameter.

The Hara Center is where the Monad seats itself. It is seen as the color Amber. The Center is enveloped by a larger bubble of energy, the size of a soccer ball, which the Chinese call the Tan Tien (pronounced dan dien). Literally translated Tan Tien means "the field of the elixir of long life and wisdom." It stores energy then acts as a pump to move the energy through the body in a figure of eight flow. The hara lines provide the energy to fill the Tan Tien. The hara center is a reservoir for the original spark of energy that was formed through the combination of sperm and ovum to create the zygote. The Hara Center holds a

unique vibrational note that holds our body in the physical manifesta-
tion. When this note vibrates at the same frequency as the core of the
Earth, we are grounded. When this note stops vibrating, our body dies.
As we change its vibration, our life circumstances change.

If we have dysfunction here, we feel driven to control. We feel inse-
cure or unsafe. We perceive unfairness everywhere. We react by becoming aggressive (bullying) or submissive (victim). We often feel under
attack and hence feel a need to defend against others or the world in
general. Assertion, along with empowerment, can naturally replace aggression, or victimization, when the Hara Center is functioning at optimum levels. The connection to one's inner authority is restored. We
resume our connection with the Earth's power. It gives us access to true
power and courage.

Diaphragm Chakra

The Diaphragm chakra is located near to the diaphragm muscle, just
above the Solar Plexus. It is seen as Olive green (blend of yellow and
green). Functionally it provides for clearing. It can be quite an intense,
deep, emotional purging. Indeed, it is sometimes referred to as the
'vomit' chakra'! The process is ultimately positive, but may not seem so
at the time. Go through it by simply allowing it to happen. Watch the
sensations, then let them go. Avoid fighting, resisting, or trying to
change them. Welcome the clearing. Send love. (This clearing is what
was happening to the baby I mentioned in the previous section. It is
why the mother vomited.)

Thymus Chakra or Soul Seat

The Higher Heart Chakra, sometimes termed the Thymus chakra, is
the same energy center I term the Space of Pure Potential.

This chakra is located on the breastbone approximately three inches
(7.62 centimeters) above the nipples. It is seen as deep teal in color.
According to Diane Stein in her book *Psychic Healing with Spirit Guides
and Angels* this chakra connects the Hara line and emotional body to

the Kundalini line and etheric subtle body. On the physical level, this chakra protects the immune system, which is clearly affected by the emotions. On the emotional level our wish to live, to maintain this incarnation. This center holds our drive and passion to fulfil the task we incarnated to accomplish in this lifetime. It is a vital center utilized for profound healing. Human Design's originator Ra Uru Hu, describes the Higher Heart as containing a magnetic monopole that enables us to tap into the Law of Magnetism and the Law of Attraction and draw to us those people and synchronistic experiences that we need in order to fulfil our purpose. This is another way of describing the SPP resources we have been discussing. The Higher Heart is also where our Higher Selves connect with us.

When you find the location, you will know immediately, it is painful. Sensitive to pressure. Gently pressing this point brings us fully awake to the grief we have historically carried.

It connects us with the vastness which awaits as merciful awareness. Meditating on the sensations that come while touching this point opens us up in order to release grief (which may include anger, resentment, fear or other feelings.) Tapping this point has been called 'The Thymus Thump.' This simple procedure will activate the Thymus gland.[4]

Our Soul connection, sometimes called the silver cord, connects into the back of this chakra. Within the soul seat lies our passion for who we wish to be. For what we have come to accomplish in this life: our Spiritual longing.

Dysfunction here enables us to stop feeling the deep pain of our human experience. We have deep heart/emotional issues (sadness or grief perhaps), yet we are unable to access them, or know how to mourn. We feel numb. We walk through life as if we are sleepwalking or under anesthesia. We can experience wounding around the loss of the ability to experience pleasure in our physical bodies.

Only by mourning the losses in our lives are we able to transform the numbness. We may then truly access the power of our own hearts, our immense ability to be truly compassionate, to unconditionally love.

Dysfunction here means that we have no sense of purpose or what we want to do with our lives. Drifting along, sometimes depressed, having given up because of not caring.

We are unable to connect with others if this chakra is dysfunctional. Shrouding here is energetic. It represents stuckness. I often assist by removing the shrouding. My own understanding of the Space of Pure Potential, as I refer to this chakra, unfolds through the rest of the book.

Individuation Point Chakra

The Individuation Point (Sometimes called the Transpersonal point or the 9th chakra) is located centrally above the head, usually positioned where you can reach with your outstretched hand. Above here is Unity, below it we perceive separateness. The Individuation Point enables a connection with the universe. It supports enlightenment, together with ascension. The transpersonal point separates the soul aspect embodied in human frame as you, from the rest of your Soul. Thus giving you a personal reality while living your earthly life. You perceive yourself as separate, even though you are still very connected to your Soul, your Monad (your Souls' Soul), and Eternal Source.

When there is dysfunction here we cannot seem to transcend our human experience or access the Soul level of our being. We struggle with our God Image, along with issues around that concept. We are cynical. We never ask the question "isn't there more to life than this?" Pure materialists are often disconnected at this point.

It is very important to develop both the **Individuation Point** and the **Earth Star** simultaneously rather than separately. Working on aligning the whole haric energy system assures this.

Earth Chakra (s)

The Earth chakras are also known as sub personal chakras or the Earth Star chakra. According to Diane Stein the location of these centers is fifteen centimeters below the feet, within the Earth's surface.

Diane believes that the Earth Chakra anchors the incarnation and purpose into the earth plane reality, makes earth one's home. It is through this chakra that we receive the terrestrial/telluric energy, rising through the chakras of the feet. The story of our lives (our karma) is recorded inside of the matrix of our Earth Star Chakra.

Some yoga tantric specialists describe a total of five sub-personal chakras. These being located below the Muladhara, or Root Chakra, and above the Earth Star Chakra.

These five sub-personal chakras are numbered from the nearest one to the body, a few centimeters below the feet, to the fifth one, two arms lengths below the feet. I have listed them and their relation to the hara lines. They are:

1. **Incarnation Point Chakra:** located a few centimeters below the feet. Practical implementation of the Soul's journey for the current life. Affiliated with hara Line 5 as HL5 is associated with Life Purpose.
2. **Incarnation Chakra:** about 15.5 inches (40 centimeters) below the feet. Connection to ancestry, tribe, clan. Affiliated with Hara Line 3's purpose.
3. **Sub-personal Leadership Chakra:** below the feet at an arm's length. Connection with the female archetype. Affiliated with Hara Line 6.
4. **Earth Centering Chakra:** below the feet at just over an arm's length. Links to the archaic earth energy. Affiliated with Hara Line 1 and 2.
5. **Earth Star Chakra:** below the feet at two arms' length. Exchange and relationship with the Earth Goddess. Affiliated with Hara Line 1 and 2.

At the end of earthly existence, we disconnect from the Earth Star and climb through 'the tube of Light', which is in fact the Hara Line Balance Connection, and we pass through all the hara line chakras.

When we arrive at the Crown and see ahead of us the Light from the

Soul Star, we are perceiving the 'tunnel' and the light mentioned by those who have had 'near death experiences' (NDE). In the process of this ascension, we perceive our whole existence, ordered from the beginning to the end. This is the life review experience many people who experience an NDE talk about.

The Core Star

The Core Star is located in the center of our being behind the solar plexus area. It is our individuated God-self.

When open and functional it radiates divine light out into our environment. It is more often than not closed, partially closed, or radiating at less than optimum levels. It may be restored to optimum function with the assistance of the Higher Self if the person is ready for the change.

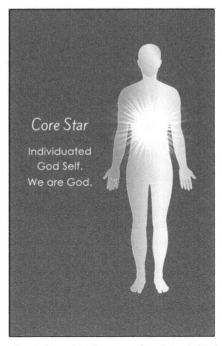

Figure 32 - The Core Star is located in the center of our being behind the solar plexus area.

My guides tell me there is more detail to come in due course. For now, this is adequate. In reality these energy centers are much more complex.

The Universal Ordering Service is open

Let us spend a few moments discussing the subject of setting a Goal. You could call it the Universal Ordering Service. You place your order and trust it will be delivered.

As with all things there is a right way and a wrong way to do this. This SMART goal setting method, I learned during my NLP training many years ago. I'm a Certified Trainer of NLP. Each time I've taught it the students experience a lot of ah ha's and then understand why their goals remain unattained most of the time.

Figure 33 – The SMART acronym to aid goal setting.

SMART is an acronym for Specific and Simple, Measurable and Meaningful, As if Now (in the way it is stated), Achievable, Realistic, Responsible, Timed and Towards.

SPECIFIC means as much detail as possible. For example, I want to be happy is not specific. I am happy to have graduated from college with the Degree I wanted, is specific.

SIMPLE means write it down in simple language, using a minimum number of words. Writing it down is crucial to manifesting. Write it down so that your unconscious mind can understand clearly what you want. Write it as you would do to make it clear for a bright, nine-year-old child.

MEASURABLE means you can chart your progress by implementing assessable steps. You must have an evidence procedure so you know when you have reached your goal.

MEANINGFUL means that you must have the energy of a positive high vibe emotional investment like passion, to support you and aid the Law of Magnetism.

ACHIEVABLE means you must believe it's possible to attain this goal in the time frame you have chosen. You could also add *accountable* here in that if you ask someone to hold you accountable you will most likely find it easier to stay committed and on track.

AS IF NOW means it must be written down in present tense as if its already happened. This is because there is only NOW. Plus, the unconscious mind will take the path of least resistance, and hence keep the goal forever in the 'future' unless you state a specific time frame.

REALISTIC means that it must be possible for you. That you are capable.

RESPONSIBLE means harm no one, be aware of ecology, the impact on others. For example, never try to acquire what is rightfully someone else's like their spouse, job, or money.

TIMED means a realistic time frame is crucial, preferably stating the month, day, and year of achievement.

TOWARDS means that goals need to be 'towards motivated' rather than 'away from' motivated. We've covered this concept of 'towards and away from motivation', in detail already, therefore you know why this is important.

If you wish to ensure your chance of success to be the highest possible, may I suggest you adhere to the following:

- Ensure congruency of your personal beliefs with the goal
- Be accountable
- Take action
- Be committed
- Ensure haric alignment of all hara lines, especially:
  o Hara Line One (be in 'now' where the power is)
  o Hara Line Two (access to your power of intention)
  o Hara Lines Three and Four (you need to be able to receive graciously)
  o Hara Line Five (you need to believe yourself worthy and deserving of receiving)
- Use your imagination in order to have an internal picture of yourself having attained your goal on the date specified
- Be aware that the Universe will deliver even if it's in a package slightly different to your expectation
- Write down your goal in a way that conforms to the SMART criteria

The big temptation people have, after placing their order with the Universe, is that they decide to change it. Or they are unable to trust the process and start having doubts. Just remember, if you are hungry and want your food to be brought to you quickly, then it's best not to change your food order with the waitress a few minutes after the chef started to cook for you. Your job is to place the order with the Universe and then let go of 'how' it will come to pass. When you order online do you trust the company to arrange delivery? Yes, of course you do. Do you try to interfere with the delivery service, certainly not if you want your goods timeously.

Example of a Written Goal
It is (date) and I am (positive emotion) because I have achieved my goal of (specify).

Review
- A state of mind is different to a goal. A state is something you can immediately have. A goal is time based.
- There can be short, medium, and long terms goals. All of which may support an overall 'Outcome.'
- All goals require imagination in order to have an internal picture of the outcome. See yourself in the future feeling the emotions attached to having attained what you want.
- Goals can be sabotaged by limiting beliefs. Therefore, it is important that any beliefs around not deserving, not being worthy, not being good enough, victimhood and so on are addressed and released before setting the goal.
- You can only set goals for yourself, never for others

Enlightenment and The Space of Pure Potential
As I have already said the Space of Pure Potential (SPP) exists within each human. It is where we access the main Zero Point within us. I wish to be careful not to place limits around this space or the concept of it, by defining it or naming it anything other than the Space of Pure Potential (SPP). As I've mentioned its color is teal or deep turquoise.

I call this area the Space of Pure Potential because Enlightenment lives here. Enlightenment is a state of no emotional burdens. Freedom from the pull of the past or fear of the future. It's a state of being secure, gracefully, happily in the present, with a childlike trust in the future. The only way to know this space is to experience it.

A 'near death experience' NDE, is a taste of the enlightenment state. In that experience a person is spontaneously released of all emotional burdens. Similar, even if less intense states, are accessed when high school graduation exams are successfully finished. Tremendous relief. It's usually fleeting. Very soon the exhilaration is gone when it is realized college is next together with its own exams and challenges. For a brief moment however, there is relief.

Everything connects with the SPP. There are various deliberate ways to get into the field of Pure Potential. However, it must be mentioned here that just about everyone has already had the experience of being in that space without realizing it. For example, when mothers and babies are bonding through gazing at each other, they both naturally access the SPP. It is the space of pure love. It is also spontaneously accessed after loving coitus. Also when lovingly stroking a special pet. During certain types of body movement like rhythmic swaying, various types of chanting, or stillness with focus on an object of meditation. Experienced meditators often have the goal of accessing the SPP. Kriya yoga body movements, or pranayama breath control, also give access to the SPP. Any activity, thought or movement that changes focus from outward to inward takes you into the SPP. Acts of altruism do it too. Going into SPP takes us from segregated to connected.

Let me give you a brief experience of the SPP right now.

Just stop. Can you remember a time when you felt joyful, relaxed, happy and loved? Notice how you feel. You are now experiencing a small taste of the SPP.

An Example of the Use of the SPP in Action

Sally told me an interesting story of the SPP in action. She rides horses. The experience took place when one of them needed re-shoeing. The farrier was in a bad mood. The horse was obviously picking up on the farrier's mood. It was getting unsettled. Sally had to think on her feet. She just said to the farrier "when was the last time you did something you really enjoyed that brought you joy." Immediately the farrier's mood changed. The horse quickly settled down.

Animal communicators have to access the SPP in order to commune

with animals. Successful Animal Trainers operate from the SPP, because when a person is in that space of pure love no animal feels threatened, just connected. If, when a person is fearful, you are in SPP in
their presence, they will soon begin to feel safe. Being in SPP allows us
to influence the energy of others in a positive way. The SPP is a magnetic center that allows us to influence the energy of others through
compassionate connection. Just by being in the SPP we get insights for
healing. Both for ourselves and others.

If you are a healer who wishes to use the SPP to enhance your practice methods, it's important not to 'act' as a healer. There is a need to
go beyond 'you' into the NOW where you may connect with the SPP.
Then anything becomes possible in the gentle, profound space, around
the Higher Heart /Thymus Chakra.

Awareness together with being in SPP creates community. Imagine
everyone on the planet in their SPP, naturally connected to everyone,
to everything. How beautifully transformative that would be.

When everyone is in their own SPP the top down type of Dictatorship is redundant. Each person intuitively knows their role just like bees
in a beehive as we have discussed. No one is in charge yet everyone
knows how to function in support of the whole.

Quieting the mind through meditation supports moving into your
center. When one moves into the magnetic center of the physical body
the turbulence of the active part of the mind is shielded, discounted, or
nullified.

Place your focus in the center of the magnetic energy generated by
the heart-beat. The wave produced by the magnetic energy of the heart
beat, is much stronger than the waves produced by the brain (i.e. alpha,
beta, theta, delta, gamma) therefore, it is insulating in effect. The mind
is instantly quieted. We are buffeted by all the mental energy, of self
and others, when not in SPP. We are quiet when in it. There is ease
and effortlessness in one's understanding. From this point one's ambi-
tious self is curtailed. This allows better health of the community, engenders less selfishness or competition. It supports 'others' rather than

'self' being pushed to the forefront. It engenders Esprit de corps.[5] Service to others before service to self.

Entering into the SPP, together with balancing and aligning your energy system enables:

- You to find happiness, fulfilment
- To switch into your life purpose
- To tap into your own power of intention in order to co-create effectively
- Re-connects you back into The Divine Gridwork of the Universal Mind (the Unity, Christ or Krystos Grid)
- Re-connects you to Mother Earth
- Assists in the re-alignment of the Hara Line; life just works
- Unblocks or repairs the energy system on multidimensional levels
- Aids mental, emotional, physical, and spiritual healing
- Helps identify, then release, karmic issues
- Builds a deeper soul connection

Merely intent and focus from the heart is enough to encourage changes!

Get out of the head. Shut 'off' the head. Turn 'on' the heart.

My task, through the teachings of this book, is to engender awareness of the need to build a heart-based connection in all of us through the awakening of the SPP.

Space of Pure Potential Exercise and Meditation

Let's first find out where you are.

Close your eyes.

Now imagine you are standing in front of a mirror looking at your reflection in a way that is different to when you have your eyes open. Allow yourself to become aware of where your inner sight comes from. Is it somewhere within your body? Or without? Where exactly?

That is where your consciousness is currently residing.

Now, create a miniature version of yourself with arms and legs and eyes and mouth, and then let's begin our journey to discover your personal space of pure potential.

Can you remember a time when you felt joyful, relaxed, happy, and loved? (This will begin the process in a gentle way).

Now imagine you are stepping out of the front door of your home. Exit your home and if you live at an above ground level find yourself changing location if necessary, so that you are walking on the ground.

Imagine from there you have found a pathway. Notice what you are walking on, what do you sense? What can you feel under your feet? Maybe you can hear your steps on the ground, perhaps see the way ahead. Maybe you smell something pleasant in the air.

Follow the pathway as it turns to the right. Notice your perfect place is ahead. It has an attractive doorway which is located up three steps, you feel drawn to enter.

Ascend, the three steps, 1, 2, 3 across the landing, then when you are you ready, open the door and step in through the doorway. What do you notice? Maybe you feel differently as you enter this special place. Perhaps there's a feeling of sinking, pressure, spreading, expansion, calmness, peace, relaxed, in the zone, womb-like, quiet, blissful, or satisfied. Or something else. Just notice the difference, however subtle. Maybe there is color if so, notice what the color is.

Stay here for as long as you wish then return to full consciousness while simultaneously holding onto the stillness.

After you become practiced in entering the SPP, become extremely familiar with the experience of residing in your SPP, you may wish to use your favorite one of the following shortcuts:

All shortcuts are down.

1. 1, 2, 3 be there, in your SPP.
2. Imagine yourself as a stone being thrown into a wonderful safe pool.

3. Imagine you are on a feather floating to your SPP.
4. Imagine you are experiencing a snow run luge downward into your SPP.
5. Simply set the intention to go the SPP
6. Go to the center into the stillness. Just like in a storm the eye is the quiet place. Go to center. The center is peaceful, still, quiet.

The next method is excellent for Thinkers rather than visual people.

Think of a spiral staircase leading from an upper room to a lower room you call the great room. There are 12 stairs downwards (4 multiples of 3). Make your way easily down the stairs.

The Higher Self

In the Huna system, the Higher Self, (sometimes known as the Angel of the Presence), is termed the Superconscious Mind. (You may wish to review the prime directives of the Superconscious mind that we discussed earlier). It is the aspect of us that acts as an intermediary between our physical being and our Soul while we are in earthly incarnation. The vibrationary rates of the physical body, Higher Self, Soul, Oversoul/Monad[6] are different. The physical vibrates at a lower level than the Monad which vibrates at the very highest level. Each level increases in vibrationary rate. Only things that have the same vibrationary rate can communicate or magnetically attract each other. The vibration of the Physical body must be raised considerably before the Soul can connect with it directly. Hence the role of the Higher Self as a stepped down vibration or bridge between physical being and soul being.

The Higher Self is an agent of healing. It is a totally trustworthy guardian and parental spirit. It patiently waits for us to ask for its assistance.

Many people are unaware of the existence of their Higher Self. The Higher Self sees our life from a different, higher perspective. The Higher Self is fully aware of our life purpose, together with what we have experienced thus far in life. The Higher self is our loving parental guide. It has our best interests at heart. Many people are walled off from their Higher Selves. They push the energy of the Higher Self away. They ignore the promptings of the Higher Self.

How to Connect with Your Higher Self

To connect with your Higher Self is very simple: you just intend it. Then you issue an invitation. Then go into your SPP and make a request to your Higher self to draw closer to you. The request is best spoken out loud. Sometimes when we 'think' something we are not as focused as when we speak out loud. You may use the symbol I created for strengthening your Higher Self connection if you wish.

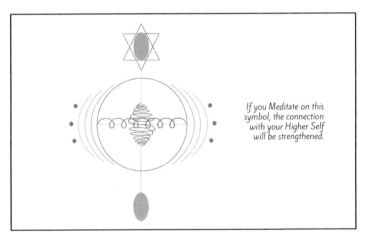

If you Meditate on this symbol, the connection with your Higher Self will be strengthened.

Figure 34 - Higher Self Connection meditation symbol.

Review
- You have an SPP use it wisely
- You have spiritual selves – learn to connect with them
- You have the ability to connect with multi-dimensionality through your hara lines
- Hara Line re-connection causes health and evolution to occur
- Emotions are not Dictators they are messengers
- The seven Hara Lines are the 7 Keys to Health, Harmony, Success and Abundance

- Abundance consciousness is a choice
- Goal setting is a skill that is easily acquired
- Lines of contagion enable connection
- Energy is the source of change, growth, or stagnation
- Your Energetic Precedence always precedes you and others can read it
- Your Core Star is where your individualized 'Godself' resides

CHAPTER 6
FINDING LOVE

We are fundamentally and deeply connected
with each other, and with the planet itself.
– ROLLIN MCCRATY PH.D.,

I HOPE I HAVE now given you enough evidence to show not only that we are all connected, but *how* we are all connected. Also, how emotions affect health. How our environment either supports health or induces ill health. How science has proven energy healing works. How our cells have consciousness. How physics has proven metaphysics and philosophy to be valid models of our world. How multiple dimensions can exist. How energy can be retrieved from space, the omnipresent stillness, to save raping the planet. How sustainability, along with health, can be supported by our understanding of, and living within, nature's divine design. And, how water has memory.

We are all familiar with electrical energy. With wiring diagrams. With all the paraphernalia such as junction boxes, circuit breakers, transformers and fuses that are required to harness electrical power, for use in our homes and factories. The human body has similar wiring that enables us to function through the flow of bio-magnetic electrical currents of energy.

If you needed some electrical wiring repaired in your home would you call an electrician or a plumber? Naturally you would call an electrician. A person skilled to do the job. When humans experience lack of energy flow they need someone skilled in energy healing to help them remedy the problem. The average family doctor or a hospital surgeon usually knows nothing of meridians (think energy channels or 'wiring') and chakras (think 'circuit breakers or junction boxes'). Doctors are skilled for the Emergency Room. They function best in life and death situations. Chronic conditions are often due to energetic stagnation, emotional insults or toxicity. It makes sense to call in the right person for the job.

'Reality' is not as simple as we have been led to believe.

The human nervous system can sense the energy all around us. As we have discussed this energy is sometimes referred to as background energy or energy from the vacuum, omnipresent stillness. In truth we now know there is no vacuum if energy is present. The space around us is teeming with infinite possibilities that we can interact with, consciously or unconsciously, to attract, or resist, those situations and people we either want to be with or want to avoid.

The Field

Lynne McTaggart's book, *The Field*, provides a scientific explanation for psychic phenomena such as extra sensory perception (ESP), spiritual or energy healing, or remote viewing.

It explains that everything is connected. Terms such as Morphic Resonance, Morphogenic Field, Morphogenetic field, have been coined to name this field of connection. As well as Zero Point Field (ZPF). Lynne describes a sea of energy that reconciles mind with matter, classic science with quantum physics, and science with religion.

The ZPF is "a cobweb of energy exchange" as Lynne describes it.

The Field has inspired thousands of people from various walks of life. Including religious leaders, physicists, and healers. Perhaps most important of all, those who have been seeking scientific evidence for their innate sense that they are not separate, that they do not live in isolation from others or the Earth.

The SPP is obliquely referred to by others. For example, Dr. Deborah Rozman, the President of Quantum Intech, has said "Research findings have shown that as we practice heart coherence, radiate love and compassion, our heart generates a coherent electromagnetic wave into the local field environment that facilitates social coherence, whether in the home, workplace, classroom or sitting around a table. As more individuals radiate heart coherence, it builds an energetic field that makes it easier for others to connect with their heart. So, theoretically it is possible that enough people building individual and social coherence could actually contribute to an unfolding global coherence."

She continues "The word coherence means order, structure, alignment within and amongst systems. This applies to organisms, human beings, social groups, planets or galaxies. This harmonious order signifies a coherent system whose optimal functioning is directly related to the ease and flow in its processes. Basically, feelings of love, gratitude, appreciation and other 'positive' emotions not only have an effect on our nervous system, but they have an effect on those around us, far beyond what we might have previously thought."

My Big TOE

Physics is related to, indeed derived from, metaphysics. Tom Campbell has said, "*My Big Theory of Everything* describes, as it must, the basic oneness, continuity and connectedness of All That Is. It systematically and logically describes the natural relationships between mind and matter, physics and metaphysics, love and fear, and demonstrates how time, space and consciousness are interconnected; all with a bare minimum of assumptions (that are so prevalent in most scientific theories). It resolves a host of longstanding scientific, philosophical and metaphysical problems."

Tom states that Consciousness is the computer. Physics is related to and derived from metaphysics. Mind consciousness and the 'paranormal' are given a scientific explanation. He goes on to say "The evolution of knowledge demands that sooner or later truth must succeed, and falsity must self-destruct. Although the consensus of culturally empowered opinion may carry the day, measurable results will carry the day after that. Only truth can produce consistent results. In contrast falsity excels at producing assertive beliefs, arguments, and opinions. Open your mind, remain skeptical, pursue only significant measurable results, and let the chips fall where they may. Culturally conditioned mental reflexes need to be re-examined, generalized, and expanded. Think out of the box, out of the ball-park, out of the Universe as well."

As Tom says "Modern science and technology are only now providing the combined knowledge by which metaphysics can be understood. The nature of reality has both a subjective and objective component."

The advice he gives is to explore the reality-wilderness. Because 'Big Truth', once understood and assimilated, always modifies your intent. This invariably leads to personal change.

Ask any top-notch athlete if focused intentional mental preparation is important to his or her success.

Tom runs over cherished cultural beliefs because he unifies Physics (what we think of as objective, or normal) with Metaphysics (what we consider subjective, or paranormal). He morphs Theology to Philosophy. He postulates that we must accept some things with uncertainty because "proof is only for whiskey." Therefore, impossible when it comes to science. Evidence is acceptable to science in the form of results.

People's subjective experiences of healing isn't proof to anyone else. However, the person's healing success story as evidence may give hope to many. The only way you will know if this will work for you is to follow my guidelines. Then you will have your own subjective experience. This will then form your own proof.

What Is Love

I see Divine God Source Eternal Supreme One, Eternal Source, Creator Source, the All That is, Prima Materia, First Cause, or God if you prefer, as Divine Creative Intent. The Unity divided itself into two and the created aspect became responsible for creating everything else.

Many, including Deepak Chopra have said God is a verb, rather than a noun. What we call God is a process. The process is loving-kindness. This is highly simplified. Few of us are conscious enough to understand what God is beyond this.

Love is unqualified giving. If we wish to engage with this form of love, we must open our hearts fully. Naturally this is a scary prospect. Deeper exploration of the heart means going into an area we perceive as unsafe. It is our own fear of completely, unreservedly, giving and receiving Love that causes us to feel separate from the unified loving-kindness. It is blasphemy to believe God is a separate being from you. Maybe we are all afraid of rejection because we have already rejected our true selves.

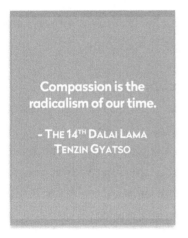

Compassion is the radicalism of our time.

- THE 14TH DALAI LAMA TENZIN GYATSO

The created multi-verses began with a separation of opposites, the tearing apart of the united opposites. The late Itzak Bentov[1] did a wonderful job of explaining the nature of creation in his lectures. Read his book *Stalking the Wild Pendulum, Mechanics of Consciousness.*[2]

Inside each of us there is both a so-called heaven and a so-called hell. There is an inner universe, just as there is a universe outside of us. All the order, together with all the chaos, of the universe, exists inside each of us. We are a fractal.

Within the time frame of the last 228,000 years, humanity has been manipulated, both genetically and psychologically, by non-human heartless, soul-less, off-world Archons[3] in order to achieve their hidden agenda; to devolve humanity into a primitive, savage, enslaved race, complete with transhuman DNA. We were originally created as Twelfth Dimensional Liquid Light Beings. More angelic than physical. We need to evolve ourselves, one person at a time, back into fully heart-centered consciousness. We then reclaim the full Divine Template for the advanced, loving, benevolent race, we were originally divinely designed to be.

> Love is a sacred reserve of energy.
> It is like the blood of spiritual evolution.
>
> - PIERRE TEILHARD DE CHARDIN

My belief is that a healer's job is to identify disconnectedness, in order to then reconnect and effect liberation. This applies both to self and clients.

My goal is to engender Unconditional love for all beings, by all beings. This is what I, along with many others are working for. It's that simple.

What Is Unconditional Love?

Unconditional love means you love and accept someone regardless of their behavior, while not necessarily condoning what they do.

Enabling, on the other hand, is acting in a way that allows the loved one to continue behavior that is damaging to either themselves or others. It is often easier to be an enabler than to hold someone responsible for their behavior. However, 'easier' is the wrong choice.

Love Is Often Understood by Living in a Situation Where There Is a Lack of It

This is what Osho had to say on love and compassion:

"When it comes to love three things are to be taken note of. The lowest love is sex—it is physical—and the highest refinement of love is compassion. Sex is below love; compassion is above love; love is exactly in the middle. Very few people know what love is. Ninety-nine percent of people, unfortunately, think sexuality is love, it is not. Sexuality is very animal; it certainly has the potential of growing into love, but it is not actual love, only potential.... Sex is the seed, love is the flower, compassion is the fragrance."

Buddha defined compassion as 'love plus meditation.' When your love is not just a desire for the other, when your love is not only a need, when your love is sharing, when your love is not that of beggar but an emperor, when your love is not asking for something in return but is ready only to give, to give for the sheer joy of giving, then add meditation to it and the pure fragrance is released. That is compassion; compassion is the highest phenomenon."

Letting Love Flow

Love can only flow into and out of the hearts of those people who have not made a conscious or subconscious decision to block it, or not allow themselves to receive and give. Everyone seeks love because Love is our natural and eternal state. The illusion, however, is that it can only be found in the form of being given by others. People are often unaware that we have love within us. Firstly, understanding this, then secondly, acceptance of that Love within, is a major step forward. Moreover, it is our purpose to allow love to flow freely, abundantly, to all members of humanity. In this state of compassion, of unconditional love, our energetic precedence, our entire energy field, expands infinitely. This is opposite to its other state of being small, compressed, close to our physical body. When all Energetic Precedencies meld or entangle in love, the energy field of humanity, along with the Earth, enables an attitude of harmony and co-operation. This is a healthier opposite to the usual divisiveness, xenophobia, bigotry, racism, or conflict.

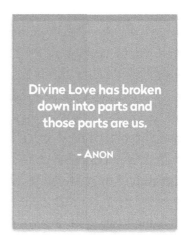

Divine Love has broken down into parts and those parts are us.

- ANON

When energy fields meld together, we feel more of the oneness that we really are. It becomes almost impossible to continue creating separation. Or to continue believing in the illusion of isolation. In fact, the only way we can continue to accept the idea of non-connectedness, is when we block the flow of love, and ignore the truth of entanglement, by intending to separate our individual physical form, in order to take complete control over it. Or, in order to hide our true nature from ourselves or others. People develop 'Parts' of themselves that have become detached from their wholeness. These little 'Sub Personalities' battle for control, create inner, and/or outer, conflict. They become players in the illusionary game of a fearful reality of separation that is destroying human society.

Disagreements almost always escalate because of egoic posturing, or mis-perceptions due to our filters. The Ego lives in fear rather than in love. That is the way it is. The Ego was originally given to us by the Archons to make three-dimensional life more readily assimilated. Also to make us easier to control through the emotion of fear.

The Ego resides within the unconscious mind and directly communicates with the conscious mind. A consequence of the unconscious mind's design, is that we have access to our imagination, are free to be creative, to explore, to learn, to grow, and to evolve out of the 'illusion' we call 3D reality. The Ego is not wise like the Super Conscious mind. Egos are designed to do their tasks within the confines of a special area of the mind. However, they often get involved in areas where they have no right to be. That's of course when the fun starts. Because our egoic in-built fear encourages us to believe that the 3D illusion is real. We feel threatened once we start to realize that the illusion is unreal, a matrix we have been conditioned to accept. Egos tend to fear their own demise or redundancy. This is another illusion of course because taming the mind simply leads to the Ego becoming less fearful by default. The Super Conscious Mind (aka Higher Mind or Higher Self) is the mind shared with the Soul. Therefore, when the Ego releases its fear, it enables a rise in vibration. This then allows it to simply re-integrate into the higher vibration of the wholeness of consciousness, which being ever present, has been available all along, yet inaccessible due to a mismatch of vibration.

Love is all there is. Each person is designed to be at one with that Love. Inseparable. Therefore, each person is Love. What gets in the way of realizing this is low self-worth, feelings of not deserving, insecurity or lack of trust. Therefore, some people believe it is an arrogant notion to say, 'We Are Love.' Indeed, we are in fact Divine Beings. We can only accept this truth once we have experienced the open-hearted feelings of giving, receiving, compassion or being at one with Love.

Remember:
You are who you believe yourself to be
You get back what you think you deserve

Let's discuss love's role in these two statements.

My Guides wish me to state their words "this book was written from the Space of Pure Potential. With your permission, we offer you love as a tool for you to use to heal yourself. Naturally you can take it or leave it. We offer love and only love. This is the only energy we use. We will say it at every turn to make this clear. There are no belief systems to agree to. No ceremonies. No gurus. No religion. No dogma. No cults. No Sects. Just shared love from the ubiquitous Higher Heart, the Space of Pure Potential."

Healing does not need to be hard work. Indeed, it can be effortless, easy. Whatever you choose you can create. However, you must realize you cannot just sit around waiting to be endowed with positive change. You must be the change. Get up, get out, or do something to promote it in yourself.

There are two kinds of Healers: those who create co-dependency in their clients, or those who co-create change with their clients using joint intention. Aspire to be the co-creator. Be in the SPP. Always teach your clients to reside in their SPP. That way you will empower people. They will permanently raise their vibration. In turn, they will empower others.

The cornerstones or tenets, that enable change or engender health, are: compassion and love while being fostered by community. Health is supported under these circumstances. There may be surface anger expressed from time to time one to the other, but deep compassion and love must reside at deeper levels. Compassion fosters harmony.

Love can alter anything: it is the most powerful force for change. This must be understood rather than merely paid lip service. We are infinitely changeable. Change is very easy when it is engendered in a field of love. For example, babies who never have the opportunity to bond with their carer or parent through love, suffer poor health as a consequence. Babies in Romanian orphanages[4] who have been fed, clothed, kept clean, but who have never experienced a caring touch, or been lovingly cradled or held, fail to thrive. However, as soon as they are adopted or feel loved they grow well. Love must be present for health or well-being in babies and children.

All religions promote love and compassion with the exception of Confucianism where compassion was encouraged, but not love specifically. The word 'correctness' was used interchangeably with love therefore love was never spoken of specifically. Plus, as we have learned from Osho compassion is ranked above love.

Compassion and Community

Each religion or belief system has something in common. It maybe that the followers do not acknowledge the similarities, preferring to perceive the differences. Compassion and love for example are mentioned as being positive human traits in all religions. The ubiquitous advice is 'Love thy neighbor as thyself. Do no harm. Extend a helping hand.'

Embracing each individual within the whole, creates community. Amity together with friendly relations, rather than enmity or hatred. In order to create war one must engender separateness. A person would not kill another part of himself knowingly.

The agenda of greed is a religion to some.

Confucianism for example taught that if you drop a pebble into water there will be waves moving outward that symbolize how one person can affect the environment.

The Golden Rule or the Epic of Reciprocity

There is a theme, you could call it a golden thread, woven throughout all religions:

"Do unto others as you would have them do unto you." Is there any better foundation for peace and compassion worldwide? Let's look at different scripture quotations from many world religions. Every single one in essence saying, Love they neighbor as thyself, do no harm, extend a helping hand. Do unto others as you would have them do unto you.

ISLAM

"Not one of you is a believer until he desires for another that which he desires for himself."

  (*Muhammad, 40 Hadith of an-Nawawi 13*)

and

"Do unto all men as you would they should do unto you, and reject for them that which you would reject for yourself."

  (*Mishkat-el-Masabih*)

JUDAISM

"What is hateful to you, do not to your fellow man. That is the law: all the rest is commentary."

  (*Talmud, Shabbat 31a*)

and

"Thou shalt LOVE thy neighbor as thyself."

  (*Moses, Leviticus 19:18*)

BUDDHISM

"Hurt not others with that which pains yourself or in ways that you

yourself would find hurtful. One should seek for others the happiness one desires for one's self."
(*Udana-Varqa, 5:18*)

HINDUISM
"This is the sum of duty: do naught unto others that which would cause pain if done unto you."
(*Mahabharata 5:1517*)

and

"Do not to others what ye do not wish done to yourself; and wish for others too, what ye desire and long for, for yourself. This is the whole of Dharma, heed it well."
(*The Celestial Song, 2:65*)

ZOROASTRIANISM
"That nature only is good when it shall not do unto another whatever is not good for its own self."
(*Dadistan-i-Dinik, 94:5*)

and

"Whatsoever is disagreeable to yourself do not do unto others."
(*Shayast-na-Shayast 13:29*)

JAINIST
"A man should wander about treating all creatures as he himself would be treated."
(*Sutrakritanga 1.11.33*)

BAHA'U'LLAH
"O son of man! If thine eyes be turned towards mercy, forsake the

things that profit thee and cleave unto that which will profit mankind. And if thine eyes be turned towards justice, choose thou for thy neighbor that which thou choosest for thyself."
(*Baha'u'llah, The third Leaf of the Most Exalted Paradise, Tablets*, p. 64)

SIKH
"Precious like jewels are the minds of all. To hurt them is not at all good. If thou desireth thy Beloved, then hurt thou not anyone's heart."
(*Guru Aranj Devji 259, Guru Granth Sahib*)

CONFUCIANISM
"Do not unto others what you would not have them do unto you."
(*Analects, 15:23*)

and

"If one strives to treat others as he would be treated by them, he will come near the perfect life."
(*Book of Meng Tzu*)

WESTERN SCHOOLS
"What you wish your neighbors to be to you, such be also to them."
(*Pythagorean*)

"We should conduct ourselves toward others as we would have them act toward us."
(*Aristotle, from Plato and Socrates*)

"Cherish reciprocal benevolence, which will make you as anxious for another's welfare as your own."
(*Aristippus of Cyrene*)

"Act toward others as you desire them to act toward you."
  (*Isocrates*)

TAO
"Pity the misfortunes of others; rejoice in the well-being of others; help those who are in want; save men in danger; rejoice at the success of others; and sympathize with their reverses, even as though you were in their place."

"The sage has no interests of his own, but regards the interests of the people as his own. He is kind to the kind, he is also kind to the unkind: for virtue is kind."
  (*T'ai Shang Kan Ying P'ien*)

NATIVE AMERICAN
"Do not kill or injure your neighbor, for it is not him that you injure, you injure yourself. But do good to him, therefore add to his days of happiness as you add to your own. Do not wrong or hate your neighbor, for it is not him that you wrong, you wrong yourself. But love him, for The Great Spirit (Moneto) loves him also as he loves you."
(*Shawnee*)

and

"Respect for all life is the foundation."
  (*The Great Law of Peace*)

AFRICAN TRADITIONAL RELIGION:
"A Sage is ingenuous and leads his life after comprehending the parity of the killed and the killer. Therefore, neither does he cause violence to others nor does he make others do so."
  (*Yoruba Proverb*, Nigeria)

and

"One going to take a pointed stick to pinch a baby bird should first try it on himself to feel how it hurts."
(*Yoruba Proverb*, Nigeria)

CHRISTIANITY
"Do unto others as you would have them do unto you."
(Luke 6:31)

and

"Love your neighbor as yourself."
(Matthew 22:36-40)

BAHA'I WORLD FAITH
"Lay not on any soul a load which ye would not wish to be laid on you, and desire not for any one the things ye would not desire for yourselves."
(Baha'u'llah, Gleanings LXVI, p. 128)

and

"Choose for thy neighbor that which thou choosest for thyself."
(Baha'u'llah, Epistle to the Son of the Wolf, p. 30)

THE RELIGION OF THE INCAS
"Do not to another what you would not yourself experience."
Manco Capoc, founder of the empire of Peru.

ANCIENT EGYPTIAN
"Do for one who may do for you, that you may cause him thus to do."
The Tale of the Eloquent Peasant, 109 - 110 Translated by R.B. Parkinson. The original dates to circa 1800 BCE and maybe the earliest version of the Epic of Reciprocity ever written.

Surely therefore, at their root, all religions are the same. The rest is window dressing. It's all about Love. The word "religion" comes from the Latin "religio" which means to "bind together" (like a bundle of sticks). However, today, people are divided up according to the many religions, cults or sects. Love unites.

We explored science and physics earlier, because Love and science do go together, as Physicist and Lecturer Tom Campbell[5] eloquently demonstrates in his presentation *Becoming Love*. A presentation from his books *My Big TOE* which he gives to live audiences and listeners around the world.

Love as a Solvent
The biggest challenge for us is to understand that Eternal Source energy holds the quality of love.

Love is an infinitely powerful solvent that we can use for dissolving those issues that have ceased to serve us.

Trust
Trust was the first thing that was lost in sentient beings. Sit quietly and ask to feel Eternal Source[6] Love energy. It will touch you anytime you open yourself to receiving. After all, you as a baby felt it quite naturally when being held, cuddled, or rocked.

Map of Consciousness
With thanks to Sally Reid for this synopsis of the Map of Consciousness.

In the dedication to the book *Transcending the Levels of Consciousness*, Dr. David R. Hawkins M.D. Ph.D.[7] writes, "This work is dedicated to the liberation of the human spirit from the bondage of adversity and limitation that besets mankind from both within and without."

Hawkins has discovered the "rules" of vibrational energy.

In his book, Dr. Hawkins explains the correlation between frequency to mood, or thoughts. The universal energy field of consciousness is the focus of his book and the frequencies of the energy that surround us in our world. Hawkins states that consciousness is capable of evolution by being calibrated by the energies of vibration. "Consciousness then evolves through progressive levels of power that can be calibrated as relative strength, much as is done with a light meter or any other measurement of energy waves."

Dr. Hawkins devised a chart that he calls *Map of the Scale of Consciousness* wherein he maps the various levels of consciousness and the corresponding vibrational frequency, descriptive emotion, along with the life view that one can expect if one aligns with that frequency.

According to Dr. Hawkins, emotions such as shame, fear or pride fall lower on the scale, while forgiveness, understanding, and love fall near the top of the vibrational map.

> We change the world not by what we say or do but by a consequence of what we have become.
>
> – DR. DAVID R. HAWKINS

The Map of Consciousness is therefore a very practical and pragmatic guide to understanding the evolutionary levels of consciousness to be transcended in pursuit of spiritual advancement, enlightenment, or self-improvement. It also provides a pragmatic map of the obstacles to overcome in order to achieve a more optimal level of consciousness. Calibrations do not establish truth but merely confirm it and lend additional corroboration.

Thanks to Dr. Hawkins, we now have a map to change our energy (thoughts) to more easily align ourselves, and our cell's vibration, to create what we want in life. For many people this is an amazing tool, but for others this is not enough. Change eludes them. The process of changing our inside to change our outside is too elusive.

With help, however, many seemingly impossible things happen. "The process of evolution of consciousness is accelerated by the combination of intention plus attention. But this does not take into account the relative power of the observer's level of consciousness or intention."

According to Dr. Hawkins, the vibrational level of the consciousness of the person may rise with help, therefore the rise in frequency allows the person to grow and change. If one is stuck in the lower frequencies as mapped by Dr. Hawkins, is it often very difficult to make that leap from being mired in blame, regret, or humiliation (lowest vibrations) up to the higher vibrations of serenity and bliss, on one's own. Here is where the help of another person and their intention can make a difference. The connection to another person at the spiritual level, and the vibrations of their intention, alters the vibrational frequency of the cells inside the first person, as documented by Bruce Lipton.

If we reflect on the Heisenberg principle, there is an explanation. "The influence of spiritual intention can therefore be over one thousand times stronger than ordinary intellectual effort. Thus, the spiritual devotee need not be an apologist to the skeptical materialist but instead merely explain that they are simply applying the Heisenberg principle for the betterment of self and the world."

The goal for the average human's vibration will be between 300 and 500. 500 being the optimal vibration for good health.

A level of 300-500 engenders the most cooperation and production in society as well as promoting peace and good health. Any higher than 500 and humans would not produce. They would not have the motivation.

If we take all the humans on the Earth, today's average human vibration is a very low 100. Poisonous food, war and other factors bring it down. The prevalence of guilt and shame also being a factor.

David makes the point that the log figures shown are logarithmic and not arithmetical. i.e. 350 on this scale is not absolute but it is 350 to the power of 10. Therefore, a small increment is really a huge increase in magnitude.

The Map of Consciousness was developed via kinesiology, or muscle testing over 250,000 calibrations spanning thirty years of multiple research studies. In his book *Power v Force* David dedicates two full chapters to the explanation of the methodology, testing, and interpretation of his Map.

Within this Map, there are a total of seventeen different levels of consciousness demarcated by different points on the scale. Moving from 0 to 500 mark a progression in the change of one's world view from a fear-based consciousness, to a love-based consciousness.

Consciousness Map Precis

GOD PERCEPTION	LIFE PERCEPTION	LEVEL	LOG	EMOTION	
Self	Is	Enlightenment	700 - 1000	Ineffable	
All-Being	Perfect	Peace	600 ↑	Bliss	
One	Complete	Joy	540	Serenity	CONSTRUCTIVE
Loving	Benign	Love	500	Reverence	
Wise	Meaningful	Reason	400	Understanding	
Merciful	Harmonious	Acceptance	350	Forgiveness	
Inspiring	Hopeful	Willingness	310	Optimism	
Enabling	Satisfactory	Neutrality	250	Trust	
Permitting	Feasible	Courage	200	Affirmation	
Indifferent	Demanding	Pride	175	Scorn	
Vengeful	Antagonistic	Anger	150	Hate	
Denying	Disappointing	Desire	125	Craving	DESTRUCTIVE
Punitive	Frightening	Fear	100	Anxiety	
Disdainful	Tragic	Grief	75	Regret	
Condemning	Hopeless	Apathy	50	Despair	
Vindictive	Evil	Guilt	30	Blame	
Despising	Miserable	Shame	20 ↓	Humiliation	

● The beginning of Integrity   ● Optimal Vibration for Good Health

Figure 35 - Consciousness Map Precis is this author's short interpretation of Dr. David Hawkins original work which he called the Map of Consciousness.

Please note that due to copyright laws the illustration is not the actual Map. This abbreviated version is a personal interpretation.

CHAPTER 7
FINDING GUIDANCE

Be who you really are on the way in,
or you will hate yourself on the way out!
— THE COUNCIL OF TRUTH

PEOPLE CAN CHANGE ANYTHING or everything about themselves with the help of their Higher Selves. Remember, we discussed the Highest Prime Directives of the Higher Self and how to connect.

Sally intended her hair to change to white and within a year she had her wish. She believed she would be taken more seriously as a wise woman if she had white hair. In more recent times we have witnessed the fad of young women dying their hair grey or white in attempts to convey mystical power or wisdom. We are in the midst of the age of lies and deceitfulness. Psychological masks and illusionary personalities are a good example of this theme in action.

Enlightenment

Many people speak of enlightenment. The Guides shared their take on it:

Enlightenment is to not need meaning. To accept all is energy. To not box or name something in order to limit. To never anthropomorphize. To discuss energy as energy and omit the terms positive or negative. Just energy that we can influence with our thoughts or actions. We can receive it or reject it. There are no names or labels in spirit. Labels limit.

Enlightenment together with the Higher Self connection is the GPS of the Soul. You don't need to read the tea leaves!

Needing to ascribe meaning to everything is a sign of fear. Applying judgment on whether something is good or bad for one is also unnecessary. Just know that it 'just is.' Just feel. We all need to get the 'only energy' story.

Here is my own take on the question 'what does it actually mean to become enlightened?'

- First to "wake up" from the dream of living in the 3D world of materialism and the materiality perceived by the five senses and then aspire to live in 5D consciousness
- Acknowledge you are more than the physical body and your ego
- Acknowledge then connect with your Soul and Higher Self
- Become aware of, and interact with, the metaphysical world
- Consciously connect to Source and the Earth
- Become aware of the oneness of all things - 'We Are'
- Acknowledge that we came from oneness and we must stop trying to separate ourselves from Divine Eternal Source
- Become master of your emotions
- Tame your mind
- Practice self-nurturance and self-care
- Embrace your inner child because he or she is probably your first direct connection with your soul nature
- Be compassionate, kind, generous, loving
- Then eventually fuse the soul and the personality together. (I will discuss this in more detail later)

I Am versus We Are

The Guides said 'I Am' is the name given to the energy of Love.

They continued to explain how saying, 'I Am' as an affirmation with the intention of evolving has been misunderstood. It leads to empowering self-love and self-acceptance, but not to enlightenment. They insist it can only get you to the halfway point.

The next step beyond 'I Am' is 'WE ARE,' the collective consciousness. The point of individual healing is communal healing and the point of communal healing is healing of the field of physical: to save the Earth and humans.

Affirming 'We Are' gets you to real enlightenment.

Enlightenment means you are no longer limited by the 3D world. Every one of us will get there in the end.

A student once asked my Guides about how to become egoless. They responded rather briefly, a little tongue in cheek; "you die!" That's how it's done. We understand enlightenment a tenth of a second after we die.

Our real self is pure awareness, pure consciousness.

We are powerful beings because that's how we were originally created and designed to be.

The I Am Presence

The 'I Am Presence' is a synonym for Monad. 'I Am' as a noun. Versus 'I am' as an adverb, such as, I am love. There has been a fundamental misinterpretation, not as noun, but as an adverb. It is not a correct translation. The proper translation from the original Aramaic is: I embody/I carry/I hold/I present. This mis-translation happened when the Latin translation was done. The Greek translation from the Aramaic was less influenced by political intrigue. Council of Nicaea and all that.

Outdated Ceremony and Ritual

Humans function best as nature intended. Which is through the Heart-mind. Just like a human cell knows its role and carries it out without an authority figure telling it what to do.

The Space of Pure Potential is the key to positive change. If you are searching for change and seeking the path, simply holding this book, as you follow the guidance of how to go into your SPP, will enable a shift to happen. Some of you may only have gentle lessons to learn. Others may have harder lessons. However, you will be helped to the degree that's appropriate for you.

How to Enter the SPP - Revisited
If we add Intention to the power of the SPP we access healing.

SPP + I = H
Space of Pure Potential plus Intention equals healing

Caution: do not think that just slipping into SPP means all will be perfect. It's crucial to remember there must be the added ingredient of placing INTENT. Intention is accessed by ensuring Haric Alignment especially in hara lines one and two.

Procedure for Moving into SPP
Whilst there are many ways of doing this as we have mentioned, quieting the mind through meditation then moving into one's center is the simplest.

In addition to the process described on page 154 you will discover a meditation on my website www.findingtruthfindinghealth.com leading you into the SPP.

Most of us prefer incremental change because it's easier to accept. Hence the role ritual, ceremony and circumstances often played. For most people, no story equals no meaning. Over the centuries spiritual ceremonies often are expanded upon, shortened or forgotten altogether. Sometimes belief systems emerge as a result of secular, spiritual or religious ceremonial participation.

I lead people into the SPP with the absolute minimum of ceremony.

Just enough support with visualization to enable them to get into the SPP and release the issue they have chosen to release in order to enhance their lives.

Spirit First Matter Second

Energy, or 'Spirit' is present before physical matter can form as already discussed. All humans have zero points within them. Moments of potential. A vast openness. Misperceptions that have become limitations can be taken into the SPP and come out changed into something more resourceful. Big shifts can come about. Or small tiny changes. When the shifts are huge often the person goes weak at the knees and needs to sit down.

Sometimes there is a feeling of wanting to pass out. For this reason, it is advisable to either sit, or lie down, in preparation for entering the SPP when intending to enable a release.

How Can Change Be Effected in the Moment of Suspension?

In several ways:

1. Through prayer and intention (all people know this)
2. When two or more people are focused on the same intention at the same moment of time
3. Surrender – this is the best and most wonderful yet the most difficult for humans because of the connotation of 'weakness' or defeat, the word itself has. In view of this, the Guides coined the words *'Yield'* or *'Open.'*

The journey is from victimhood to pure potential.

Feelings are only information. Emotions are not meant to control humans. Humans are meant to remain in control as information is presented to them through their perceptions. If we welcome the information as a message service, it ceases to have power over us. E-motion is energy in motion. Messages that are useful to us if we will but take notice of them. Emotions are sometimes insistent on getting their message across, in the same way a small child will keep pulling at your clothes until you take notice of them.

Let's imagine we are in a moment of suspension where we have the opportunity to repair ourselves or make changes through choice. Just like when an electrical engineer takes a piece of equipment, such as a radio receiver, and strips it down in order to discover the fault. When we enter the moment of suspension, we are able to be reduced to pieces, then later re-built to function even better. We may be given a new battery power supply, a fresh mains lead, or new antennae if required. We are tuned into all the stations in order to become fully functional again.

This is a deceptively simple method of getting unstuck at any level: physical, emotional, mental, or spiritual.

In essence as a Harically aligned healer I can:

- get into my SPP,
- connect with another person anywhere in the world,
- receive a request from them to assist them to release limitations that prevent them from being their true authentic liberated self,
- set a powerful intention,
- step out of the way by yielding, and then
- changes will start to happen in the recipient.

Both parties need to let that happen. That is key. Most people, whether recipients or healers, cannot allow that to happen because they need to control.

My Guides comment:

"There is a great deal that is incorrect and misleading in the business of spirituality. Many common practices are based on messages from deceptive 'spirits', rituals, ceremony and rules, all these generally recreated by a 'gateway' human who puts themselves in charge and touts 'One must have this in order to have that.' Light language, witchcraft, wiccan and so on, are examples. A number of belief systems like Voodoo, Santeria (a pantheistic Afro-Cuban religious cult developed from the beliefs and customs of the Nigerian Yoruba people which incorporates some elements of the Catholic religion,) all utilize energies available to all, yet they have twisted and bastardized the concept to the will of ego. They have therefore weakened and twisted those energies. Love and purity will always override the bastardized energies. A true heart should never fear voodoo and the like. Only those who are weak and ungrounded are susceptible."

Guide Message on 'Protection'

Session 40 June 2017

Protection is not required when it comes to energetic forces, you merely change your vibration. If you feel yourself subject to a low vibration, then ask yourself "what is the corresponding vibration in me?' Like attracts like, so where in me is the seat of this attraction?

If you do not have the corresponding vibration then the energies you deem harmful to you will not stay, or stick, because it doesn't match your own. This also relates to so called 'negative people', (we prefer the term low vibrational people), in your life. Energy vampire types or 'Takers' cannot affect you if you are a 'Non-Taker.' Being a 'Non-Taker' is not getting into 'allowing' it's just understanding you are becoming a 'Non-Taker.'

When Humans first come to Earth as a newborn infant, they are automatically Takers, as vulnerable babies they cannot provide anything for themselves. As they grow, they need to be provided for less and less. They learn they can provide for themselves. Takers (naturally or conditioned), have never realized that they have the ability to provide for themselves. They are stuck in transition, their roots not fully attached, not able to flourish alone without help.

(Rita speaking: I have a client whose Mother has never matured out of

taking. Her daughter is her chosen provider of everything from attention, to love and support. Yet she cannot do the same for her daughter. It makes for a very dysfunctional relationship.)

The Guides recommended **Stair Step of Growth** as they termed it:

1. Release the idea that you need all things provided for you
2. Take responsibility for what is in your life because it is your creation
3. Understand you have the power to alter what you feel is not on course, or not of your soul's contract, or not of your own believing
4. Develop the clarity and knowledge to trust yourself to move in the correct direction
5. Undertake the movement

As a Healing Practitioner you may wish to notice, without judgment, where the client is positioned on this 'staircase' when they consult you.

Humans have been conditioned by others who want to take from them, to take their power. In western civilization people are programmed to be serfs, to expect serfdom. Serfdom is designed to keep people helpless and to install the need to be directed. To work for people who are powerful. People who can use that power over the workers.

This is why we speak of the Synocratic Beehive type system in comparison, where all people have their own power and work together for one means, one end. Both of these ways function. However Western Society's default state is chaos which gives rise to a belief in the need for strong leadership; military generals and colonels taking command. The beehive is based on co-operation and love and knowing what to do in the moment, without needing to be told what to do.

The Three Pillars Concept

The Guides Three Pillars concept is directly channeled and transcribed without editing. It will probably feel familiar.

We wish to impart some Guidelines, general advice, that form the cornerstones of our work. We call this ***The Three Pillars.***

Figure 36 - The Three Pillars as guidance.

Let us share some good advice to enable you to have a simple life that works rather than a chaotic one. A few suggestions to assist all humans to live a more fulfilled happy life because of a greater understanding of the world in which they live, understanding of what goes on unseen, yet often, in certain circumstances, felt or sensed.

We want to avoid the term 'laws' as in Universal Laws, even though many others speak of them that way. Since everyone has free will no one is subject to 'laws.' 'Universal Laws' attempt to explain flow and how things work. Like the flow of water is affected by gravity and how rain is affected by wind. Individuals however, are not required to follow these 'Universal Laws.' It's a personal choice to take the advice, or, instead, struggle to swim upstream.

Occasionally laws have a contradictory force to force us to swim upstream for our own benefit. Always follow your own inspiration or intuition, it will probably lead you somewhere useful.

As you have already learned, if you have read this far, constant energetic flow is crucial to good health. However, stagnancy is also part of the natural cycle, like Summer and Winter. Both are needed at the right time and in the right way.

If you wish to move to a level of greater trust, then following this guidance will assist you. Trust enables you to ask for healing help once you understand how that help will come to you. Your request will come to fruition because you are a powerful being using your power of intention in a personally supportive way.

These guidelines are related to how energy works.

A tenet is a main principle or belief, especially in a philosophical context. These are our two Tenets. Hopefully you will recognize them as they have been mentioned before in this book.

You are who you believe yourself to be
You get back what you think you deserve

Pillar One — the Physical Health of the Body

Physically we advise you to pay attention to:

Nutrition – Research the organic food production movement and basic food science. The Ayurvedic tradition offers a rich wealth of advice. You are what you eat. Food affects people in a multitude of ways. Strive for balance in all things, especially food, as you were designed to be omnivores. Sustain and nurture yourself through clean food.

Breathing – Breath is the core, at the center of many levels and layers.

Exercise – Different forms suit different folks. Team sports or running alone. Calming or invigorating. Gym or yoga.

Self-Nurturance – Balance physical and mental because there is no separateness.

Variety – Variety of experience is not as crucial as a variety of foods. However, learning and growing is supported by variety of experience.

Own your body – Treat it well through consideration and self-care.

Social harmony – Harmony or discord is your choice. Change your friends and social circle if necessary.

Love – Love is the most powerful force for change. Be kind and compassionate to others.

Community – Community rather than separateness engenders health. LOVE = COMMUNITY = HEALTH

Remember:

Food, exercise, and breathing effect both the mind and the body. *All* food creates an effect in the body. A reaction. Some reactions are more noticeable than others. For example, the effect of alcoholic drinks on the nervous system cannot be denied. Even pure foods, fresh from living plants, cause reactions, albeit mostly positive, unless there is a personal intolerance present.

Meat can be slaughtered in two ways. One involves keeping the animal calm and the other allowing the animal to feel fear in the abattoir, in which case the carcass becomes tainted with fear endorphins. The Halal and Kosher processes amongst other things seek to reduce the fear generated in the animal by utilizing quick painless methods and ensuring that the waiting animals are not witness to the slaughter.

It is advisable to calm and prepare the digestive system prior to eating. Sit down and relax to eat if possible. Avoid eating on the run.

Blessing the food prior to eating is a good idea. The intention of the blessing is to calm the mind and prepare the body to receive. It does not remove fear endorphins from the meat. Blessing food by outsourcing to others such as Rabbi, Imam, or Priest, is fine but it does not relieve us from the job of calming the mind and welcoming the food into our digestive system. Never chastise yourself or others for consuming foods or certain types of food.

Be aware of comfort eating or processing emotion through the mouth. Emotionally prompted eating is also damaging. Chewing itself can be an addiction, an attempt to calm oneself. Chewing gum. Chewing the inside of the cheeks. Chewing a matchstick or pencil, a piece of grass.

Both your physical and the mental aspects need to be nurtured. Notwithstanding that really there is no separateness of the physical and mental. In all things there must be balance.

Omnivores are designed to eat anything and everything. Indeed, a lack of variety in diet causes illness. *(Rita comment: There was once a case of a financially strapped medical student who ate nothing but the free eggs his aunt sent to him from her farm. One month after eating only eggs three times a day he became ill. The movie* Supersize Me *also revealed the dangers of too much of the wrong kinds of food. Too much of anything makes Jack an ill boy).*

Addiction to substances, foods and drink is an attempt to move from one state of mind to another (see Pillar Two). Gambling, running, climbing, consumption of alcohol, all these are attempts to move from one state of mind and into another. Our point is that you can all choose to stop being victims of your own mind.

Correct Breathing & Connection

Correct breathing is crucial to good health. One of the fastest ways to change how you feel is to get more oxygen into the brain as quickly as possible therefore conscious breathing achieves that. Long deep breaths instead of shallow short ones. A rhythmic breathing pattern is helpful.

Yogis have used *Pranayama Breathing Techniques* for thousands of years. Rhythmic breathing patterns are one hundred per cent guaranteed to calm or tame a restless mind. For some however, this type of breathing may be too intense. Those people are more suited to rhythmic body movements: running, jogging, uphill walking, yoga, tai chi or similar. These activities force the body to breathe more deeply. Better breathing is the answer.

Chanting has also been used for thousands of years to calm the mind. Chanting plus the natural change of breathing required to produce the sounds is doubly guaranteed to calm and sooth a restless mind. Take an example of a crying baby. The parent picks up the child and intuitively, instinctively, moves in a rhythmical rocking way, perhaps also humming or singing a lullaby, or making repeated gentle calming noises. Then there's rocking chairs of course. Rhythmic movement of the self in relation to the world is very calming and nurturing. A mind out of rhythm is not calm and an applied, positively influencing rhythm, will force the mind to get back into natural rhythm. Recorded *Binaural Beats* are commonly utilized these days to cause the mind to move towards a different rhythm. Some people may find this sound helpful, yet they do not suit everyone.

The key to a calm mind is to create rhythm and sustain it long enough for the mind to catch on and then the positive effect becomes undeniable.

Rhythm is contagious. Can you keep your foot from tapping as you listen to a catchy beat? The brain catches rhythm from the body. Lovers breathe in unison after a deep connection. Babies and mothers often will breathe or sigh in unison. A good positive connection with others aids the mind and the body; this is a basic truth. Just as you need food you need connection. As you need breath you need connection. Connection is the medicine you need for true health.

To breathe is to BE, and when you don't breathe you don't want to BE.

To breathe is to deserve, be good enough, be valuable. Never let your value be eroded by the words of others or by conditioning.

The breath is the beginning and the end. A cycle. A rhythm.

Breath is the driver of 'now-ness.' The breath is the connection to Divine Source, where you come from.

Because you are on Earth you deserve. Simple. If you desire it, it's yours. Most of the time the Frontal Lobe and the programmed unconscious mind gets in the way of living in abundance consciousness.

Pillar Two — Mind and Thoughts

Emotional points to remember:

- Your Mind has power over the body
- Insults both mental, emotional, and physical affect health and well-being
- Erroneous perception is counterproductive to good health therefore, work at getting a pure perception
- Pivot points are moments where perception changes instantly - be aware of them
- Consider things in the context of beginnings or endings rather than cause and effect
- An Origin, or more specifically the 'Essence of Origin' may not necessarily be a point in time
- Mind and body are not separate

Humans naturally, by default, utilize various methods to settle the mind so that the body does not follow thoughts that are debilitating. For example, addiction, schizophrenia, rigidity, refusal to see truth. All of them are debilitating.

Bio-chemical imbalance can be brought about by influence of mind. The Mind sinks into itself and entropy can occur.

Remember the Emotional Body affects change by:

a) **Dispersal** (offloading on another person). Of course, this is the least resourceful and most damaging to others.

b) **Breathing** consciously, getting more oxygen into the brain, getting natural rhythm restored. Running can be a method of choice for some or chanting for others. Rhythm is contagious.

c) **Haric alignment** (see Chapter 5)

d) **Understanding** the lesson, learning it then letting go of, or yielding, the issue

Certain body parts hold certain emotions:

- Bitterness in the bones
- Anxiety in intestines/stomach
- Anger in heart, lungs, solar plexus (upper thoracic to diaphragm)
- Trepidation in the extremities and head
- Fear caps the mind leading to poor decision making
- Over responsibility for others is held in the shoulders /spine /thyroid/hips/endocrine system /pancreas
- Guilt/shame also in the shoulders/ spine/ pancreas/ thyroid/ hips/ endocrine system
- The strength of the human is in the shoulders
- Lower back and hips are usually engaged in carrying heavy loads. Guilt can be present

The mind grows in stages. For example:

1. **A young untamed mind** is always focused on 'me' and 'now.' There can be no other perception.
2. **Maturity** is signified by altruism and empathy. Acknowledgement of the presence of others. An ability to see yourself through the eyes of another person. Eventually altruism is surpassed. Awareness of community and a sense of equality of self and others takes its place.

Methods of neutralizing and releasing issues that hold you stuck in one of these two stages above are:

a) Untamed young types are just not aware of the surroundings outside of self. The story only pertains to them. No outside influences are allowed.

Neutralizer:
Movement through the world. Action through body and deep breathing.

b) Maturity is signified by altruism and empathy. An awareness of the well-being of others.

Neutralizer:
Place yourself within a group. Get distance from yourself and take second position (see yourself from another person's perspective). Give equally to self and others. The Oxygen mask in the airplane analogy helps; put on your own mask before attempting to help others. Self and others need to have equal value.

c) Eventually altruism is surpassed and awareness of community takes its place. Equality of self and others is absolutely necessary at this stage. Putting the whole of one's attention on others is unbalanced and indicates a lack of deservedness, or acceptance, in the self. This is the most debilitating attitude to have. These types of people are the most resistant to therapy, change work and healing. Unhealthy is a person who gives all to others and naught to self, due to lack of self-worth, deservedness, or inability to accept.

This state of being is difficult to neutralize because of rigidity, entrenchment and lack of awareness of what they are doing. They may believe it's their highest purpose to be a door mat! They are beyond help.

There may be three reasons why a person finds themselves in a situation where they are unable to prevent over giving to the detriment of self:

i.   Lack of self-worth, or lack of deservedness or inability to receive or accept.
ii. They believe their best and highest purpose is to give themselves to others.
iii. They are rigid and entrenched, unaware of what they are doing.

Those who fall into category iii are beyond the therapeutic help we are offering here. They will experience a health crisis. They will often feel lost when their children grow up and move away, or when others they have been caring for, die. They will experience a full-on health crisis before they will even think of allowing or asking for help. i's and ii's will ask for help. iii's will not.

Most people get stuck in:

- Untamed mind or
- Over giving

This is an important distinction.

Mind Is Related to the Body

Most books written by Westerners speak of the mind and the body as separate because it appears easier to do so. In the Eastern traditions however the two are never separated. They are always incorporated. In the practice of Yoga and meditation the two are honored as partners. Mind is related to the body. Clearly, they are connected.

When the mind is unsettled in any direction, it doesn't matter what the truth is, the body will always follow the mind's dictate. Addictions, eating problems like bulimia or anorexia, schizophrenia or other serious mental issues happen when the body follows the mind. A less serious issue would be rigidity. An even milder issue would be the refusal to see the truth. Women, for example, who believe the best of the men who are in fact cruel abusers. Self-harming, such as cutting oneself to check if the feeling sense is still operating, is an extreme symptom of a troubled mind. The pain felt may prove the ability to feel, which may eventually lead to a sense of calmness, but of course is not helpful in the long run.

Rarely are chemical imbalances responsible for mental issues/disruption. Most often it is a bio-chemical imbalance brought about by influence of mind. The neural pathways in the brain become limited in scope. Entropy sets in. The mind sinks into itself. These are all examples of the power of the mind over the body.

The mind is only a part of the body. It is not the whole existence of life. It is possible, as no doubt you are beginning to appreciate, that through a number of ways the mind can be calmed, cleared and tamed to stop it from being a 'wild animal.' In many humans it does cause animalistic behavior!

What can one achieve when the mind is calm, as opposed to troubled or busy?

A calm mind enables 'seeing' what's happening inside the body. Seeing and knowing the truth. In addition, what's happening in the outside world may be perceived differently. Pure perception requires a calm mind.

What are you trying to perceive? You are trying to perceive your own personal individual truth. Every human being is in search of this.

Yogi's tout meditation as the way to allow perception through a quiet mind. Westerners who find meditation difficult can use our alternatives or explore various others such as using the hands to create art, being in nature, listening to high vibrational music, gazing at a beautiful uplifting painting. Keep testing until you find a good match.

Let's repeat you can use your mind to either help or hurt, it's your choice.

The whole point of the exercises we offer is to change the focus of mind to the 'now' rather than to 'me.'

You can choose to stop being victims of your mind. That's the point of this book.

Pillar Three — Energy

In the beginning there was energy (aka electricity or Spirit) and vibration.

- Energy flows in a figure of eight through the body crossing midpoint below navel (see Figure 3)
- It's important that you strive for a Healthy Energetic Precedence at all levels emotional, mental, astral, and etheric
- As your energy is, so you become
- Energy is your source of change, growth or stagnation
- Health in general is supported by energetic flow. It's hindered by stagnation

Everyone is meant to overcome echoes of the past which are held as specific vibrations within the body. Whether these echoes are from past generations, or past lives, or from a time when they were younger in this life, they can always be released.

Your old karmic issues can be seen as old unhelpful, unresourceful, repeating patterns.

Because of free will you choose your parents and in so doing you are also choosing a lifestyle, together with choosing your siblings.

Chakra imbalances can undermine health.

Karmic experiences, that have the possibility of undermining health, need to be released.

Insult versus Trauma.

An event that had a negative impact in a specific moment we like to call an *Insult*.

We have specifically chosen the word insult rather than Trauma. Trauma has a negative charge. Insult is milder and has no charge. It describes the way a person reacted in the moment, in an event. An event that negatively impacted in that moment is an insult.

Disruption of energy flow.

There are three ways to disrupt the flow of energy in the body: -

1. Mind (thoughts and inner dialogue)
2. Physical injuries (when injuries fail to heal properly it's due to emotional components)
3. Emotional injuries

A young mind prior to age seven is very malleable therefore emotional injuries only occur when the experience elicits a strong, serious, aggravated, emotional response. Otherwise the child will not absorb the emotional issues. As you mature and become more aware of the outside 3D world, less focused inward, insults, betrayal being the most commonplace, are experienced. These experiences elicit a primal or primate type response, which is 'me first, you second.'

The most common emotions that lodge in the field of the body are anger and frustration.

Here are some healthy alternatives that will assist the mind in moving from a debilitating state to a more resourceful state.

1. Imagination/Also Called Visualization

The brain does not know the difference between what is experienced, perceived as real, or what is simply imagined. Imagining doing some activity that one enjoys can create the same emotional reaction in the body as actually doing it. Pathological liars believe what they say after a while and create in their mind the reality they have lied about. It's a fact that mothers who excessively fret or worry about their children actually create the very situations, such as ill-fated accidents, they fear. If the mother of an adult child, a child she has ceased to have legal control over, and yet continues to attach to the outcome of their lives, continues to feel overly responsible or keeps the adult son or daughter tied to her apron strings, then the offspring will be dangerously influenced. The numerous fearful thoughts, imaginings, visualizations, eventually become true in the mother's mind because everything is energy, everything is spirit first, before it eventually becomes reality. Things go one step further because contagion is at work and the child actively contributes to the manifestation of the event. What would happen if this ability was harnessed to be a tool rather than a dangerous detriment? The mother must imagine joyfulness, truth, prosperity, love, graciousness, goodness, in the life of her child. Unless she wants to negatively manifest the worse possible scenario for the one she loves.

Rita gave an example of a friend who in a past life experienced a dreadful situation where she held herself responsible for the loss of life of many children. As a mother she now obsessively fears for her children. We say remember, that was then, the past, this is now! Those people who are obsessed about a Past Life experience or who are living out the fears of their parents are having to overcome ECHOES of the past. The vibrational echoes of the past keep them stuck in the now. Remember now is important. Indeed, Eckhart Tolle wrote a whole book about it, *The Power of Now*.

2. Overcome Echoes of the Past

Simply put: That was past, this is now! Simple, but not easy to resolve. Let's expand on that. There are various categories of past experiences that you may wish to release.

a) Inherited issues:

People who live out *Vibrational Echoes* from their parents during rearing or gestation, in other words inherited via their DNA, or conditioned through the use of role models, can be assisted with our simple release which takes into consideration time and space.

For example, Rita had a genetic vibrational echo located at the level of her liver. She inherited it from her father who inherited it from his mother, who in turn received it from her mother. Rita's genetic echo was from three generations ago. The echo related to a 'slight' her great grandmother experienced. Great grandmother had reacted with bitterness and biliousness. There was, thereafter, an ongoing expectation of obstacles. This trait was weak in Rita but strong in Rita's father, stronger still in her grandmother. Very strong in the great grandmother where the origin lay. The theme was: problems are to be expected. Generationally all of them were just waiting for problems to happen rather than be joyful in the moment that was free of problems. Therefore, they were manifesting the problems themselves. Rita was told to follow the pathway through the liver to the beginning in order to erase it. Invert to zero point and neutralize. When a fraction inverts it neutralizes to one. Then back to zero. Visualize it anyway you choose. The change happens immediately. The outcome of expected obstacles will no longer be inevitable. This was a mild form in Rita but it can be extreme in some people.

b) Living out one's purpose

Negative Patterns often repeatedly occur. This is how you know it's a life purpose lesson. For example, a woman repeatedly chooses the same type of man as her divorced husband or abusive father, with ever escalating consequences. Or accidents repeatedly happen until the lesson is learned. Financial issues stubbornly hang around. Relationship catastrophes are repeated.

HOW TO CHANGE...

Step back, look for the over-arching pattern, then discover what you need to learn by asking yourself, "What do I need to learn from this repeating experience?" Your reply needs to be as abstract as possible instead of taking it to the smallest form. In the case of the example where a woman repeatedly chooses the same type of man as her divorced husband or abusive father, with ever escalating consequences, she could answer that she wanted to learn that she should never talk to men. However, a more appropriate learning would be more abstract, expansive, personal, and positive. For example: I need to recognize that point when my heart tells me that a man is lying to me. This woman also needs to realize that she must learn to value and honor herself. Her life lesson could be she needs to honor her truth. Choosing abusive partners means a person is discounting their own truth.

You can also ask yourself; what is *this* behavior an example of? This form of questioning leads you to an expansive learning.

Accident prone people maybe need to learn to care for themselves physically. Or maybe learn to understand the rules of gravity!

Mismanagement of money and/or love come from the same place, the same point in the body. Money is energy. Outflow of both can be mismanaged.

Chakra Imbalance or Life Purpose Lesson?

If issues continue after chakra balancing, then it's probably a life lesson. Meditation aids the discovery of the difference between the two.

What causes people to choose the life lessons they choose? Choice. Free will. Let's be clear there is no one in authority over you. You are your own authority.

Love is often more fully understood by incarnating into a family where love is absent.

Trust is sometimes learned by being born into a family where members are untrustworthy or lack trust in others.

Review

- Pillar One: is the connectedness and community of humans. The connection of humans with their bodies with regards to nutrition, breathing, and exercise. Own your body. Treat it well. Honor and consider it. Whenever possible, choose food that is pesticide free because pesticide residue becomes toxic when consumed. Glyphosate is a controversial, often confusing, topic in every area of the world where the toxic herbicide touches crops. In March 2015, the International Agency for Research[1] on Cancer (IARC) classified glyphosate as "probably carcinogenic to humans."
- Pillar Two: is about emotions and the mind – people in relation to their thoughts or memories. Use the guidance to tame your mind and stop being a victim.
- Pillar Three: is about energy and the energetic subtle bodies. Ensure your energy is always in flow.

End of directly channeled material in this section.

An Evolutionary Fast-Track

We are very fortunate to currently be living in an Ascension Timeline. A time where the thoughts and intentions, delivered via Consciousness Stream, from our Eternal Source of sustained Light, is enabling us to achieve more than one initiation, (I prefer the term unfoldment), in one lifetime. We are being supported on an accelerated evolutionary journey. We are being prompted to shift from being ego-centric, to ethno-centric, to world-centric, then to cosmic-centric.

My initial awakening into the first unfoldment in 1991 was followed by my *Awakening Your Light Body* experience with Spirit Guides Orin and DaBen which firmly anchored me in the second unfoldment in 1996. The third unfoldment followed a few years later triggered by moving continents and starting a new life. In 2012 the new cycle supported us all. I found myself transforming with ease into the Fourth Unfoldment. The process of denominalising, then anchoring, the methodology for '*HeartMind Healing*,' together with the Council of Truth's promptings, has led me to the Fifth unfoldment.

Both Alice Bailey and Blavatsky speak of the three aspects of Personality, Soul and Monad. The Monad (the Soul's Soul), is described as Life, the sustaining force, a persevering and ceaseless devotion to the pursuit of a seen and determined objective. The soul is love and wisdom, whilst the personality is knowledge and intelligent activity.

The Monad is dynamic will or purpose but remains unrevealed until after the third unfoldment.

There are seven major unfoldments[2] that all who travel the spiritual path while on Earth, must traverse. An unfoldment is a transformation in which the perceptions change, and we 'know' and understand more deeply on a mental and emotional level. We are reborn into a new role. However, we could simply see it as an expansion of consciousness, which is what it is.

Let's take a close look at the first seven unfoldments. There are seven sub-levels between each of the seven major unfoldments.

The building of one's light quotient[3] is one of the most important factors in attaining these Advanced Spiritual Unfoldments.

According to William Meader, Humanity as a whole is approaching the first unfoldment. Chaos, together with the energy of Crisis, is the burning ground that precedes a shift. It's time for us to open our hearts. To stop hating. To start to love and accept others in their uniqueness. We finally start to take on the burden of the future. This can be likened to the 'preserve the Earth for seven generations' concept of Native American tradition.

First Spiritual Unfoldment

The Earth energy is allowed to really flow into the Solar Plexus chakra. We awaken to the fact that we are spiritual beings having an earthly experience, which gives rise to a connection with our Higher Self. We start to gain Mastery over the physical. We acknowledge the existence of the Soul. We sense the underlying unity of all things. We become aware that the Earth is alive and furthermore She is conscious. That She is our Mother for the duration of our stay on her body. We are focused on wanting to make a contribution to the welfare of the larger whole. The heart activates. We begin to abhor violence.

Second Unfoldment

This unfoldment enlivens the Solar Plexus further and begins to open the higher heart chakra. Mastery over the emotional body begins. During this process, we transcend the emotional extremes that may lead to an overly addictive life experience (such as alcohol or drug abuse). Also, the ability to forgive, and to accept without judgment, is mastered. To take responsibility. To cease to blame others. To stop living in victim consciousness. Often times, people experience a change of job, or the end of a long-term marriage or some other type of longstanding partnership, during this unfoldment. There is a need to discover one's purpose. Why Am I here? being a common question. We begin to open our hearts in a wider way to what has been termed the Living Presence, known by some as Unity Consciousness, Krystos (Kristos) Consciousness, or Christ (Chryst) Consciousness. The latter term is not meant in the Christian sense but in the Universal sense. All Masters of all spiritual paths help their students embody the Living Presence many term Christ Consciousness. Our essence wants to return to the Christed status of embodying the eternal Living Light of love. Every person who is connected to Source helps to anchor Kryst (Christ) Consciousness into Earth.

Ashayana Deane, author of the book *Voyagers Secrets of Amenti,* puts it this way: *"we should aim to 'stand in the Kryst.'* Kryst (Krist) is a word that expresses the first audible sound tones that preceded Creation. The changes of spelling occurred when the word Kryst was written in English.

Third Unfoldment

This unfoldment works primarily with the higher heart chakra. Opening it up in order that the Soul can firmly anchor, then reside there. Mastery over the mental body begins. This unfoldment requires a minimum of 56% light quotient. Within this unfoldment, some support of one's soul purpose on Earth comes under the direction of the mental faculties of the initiate. A portion of the Ego is relinquished as the 'lower will' in order to be surrendered, then aligned with the 'higher will' of the soul. There is less ego. More regulatory oversight over the cravings of the body. Less appetite for consumption. The search for right relationship is triggered. We become conscious co-creators. This unfoldment energizes both soul and personality in order that they attain the same frequency in order to enable a merge. The personality is elevated to the level of the Soul. This has been termed the beginning of the Soul Merge which continues throughout the seven sub levels of this unfoldment thus preparing us for the fourth. First contact with the Monad happens.

Fourth Unfoldment

The energy of love is being generated and expressed as the fullness of the Soul connection becomes anchored. The throat chakra becomes more activated. All the chakras open further to enable greater energetic flow. The will center moves from the solar plexus to the throat. The throat begins to express the higher aspect of Divine Will. There is a blending of spirit with will, which were previously separated. We feel inspired to express and communicate. The fourth unfoldment requires 62% light quotient.

During this unfoldment, the foundation of fear we base our existence on is relinquished. Because of this the vibration is raised, thus allowing more of the soul energy to descend into the body. The soul has mastered the physical impulses of life. Towards the end of this unfoldment the initiate is able to take the joy of life and spread it around.

Fifth Unfoldment

The fifth unfoldment requires 75% light quotient. Freedom from Cognitive Blindness. During this unfoldment, the initiate receives a new direction together with a better understanding of past occurrences within their lives. In a sense, it is a rebirth into the new following a death of the old. In the process, more of the monadic energy descends into the body. The initiate has a fully formed Light Body. Is embodied 'Divine technology.' Living organic eternal spirit, self-organizing, self-harmonizing. There is the realization of being a nerve cell of our Eternal Creator. The initiate is considered to be a Working Master.

Sixth Unfoldment

The sixth unfoldment also known as Spiritual Ascension, or becoming an Ascended Master, requires 80% to 83% light quotient. At this level there is complete freedom from the wheel of rebirth. In some cases, the Initiate will leave the earth plane and their physical body, or they may choose to remain to be of service to humanity. If they leave, then the Soul concludes its contact with the Earth.

Seventh Unfoldment

The seventh unfoldment requires a minimum of 92% light quotient. This is the final and last unfoldment that can happen while living on the physical Earth plane.

Upon reaching the seventh sublevel of the seventh unfoldment, all unfoldments stop until one leaves the physical plane. Here there is full merger with the Monad and the Logoic or seventh plane of reality. The seventh unfoldment creates a complete implosion of energy in the heart chakra. It creates a whole new unified chakra system, which is metaphorically like the creation of a new star system. The seventh unfoldment is a complete commitment to service, group consciousness, along with the relinquishing of negative ego and separateness. One becomes a concentrated point of living light. It has been referred to, esoterically, as the unfoldment of 'Resurrection.' One does not complete their seventh unfoldment until they stabilize their light quotient at the 97% to 98% light quotient level.

The fastest path to completing ascension and the seventh unfoldment is to play your Divine part perfectly! Entrainment of a lower-level initiate with a higher-level initiate, through mentoring or counselling, or just through positive influence, physical presence, or being a role model, also helps.

The third, fourth, fifth and sixth unfoldments, allow you to connect with your unlimitedness. It's now possible to integrate these in one lifetime.

In order to be the best Healer you can be, focus on the expansion of your consciousness in order to traverse these unfoldments. Achieving level three greatly assists in fully activating the Space of Pure Potential. Thereby supporting the evolution of humanity.

Birthmarks
Birthmarks are frequently a result of a significant past life wound.

A Good Death
What is a near death experience?

When people report seeing a tunnel of light and moving through it, the consciousness, the eternal within us, is in fact traveling up our own Main Central Channel, in order to leave the physical body via the transpersonal chakra, so we may return as Spirit to the Soul Plane (from whence we came).

If the Main Central Channel is functioning at less than optimal levels when the spirit leaves the body at death, the Spirit may be forced to leave the body via an orifice. If this is the case it may not be able to travel to its optimal destination in the sixth dimension. The spirit may get as far as the fourth dimension or possibly the fifth but not the sixth. You may wonder why is this important? The fourth dimension has a rather low vibration. It is the destination of spirits who transition when full of low vibrational emotional issues such as guilt, fear, shame, or hate, to mention just a few. The fourth dimension may be perceived as an unpleasant place full of suffering and delusion. It is the Astral Plane of Earth. It's also the location of Archontic Invader False Light Artificial Intelligence structures and a False Ascension Matrix. Definitely a place to avoid if we have a choice. The fifth dimension is a much better destination where we can be supported, cared for, taught to learn the lessons from our earthly experiences, and experience healing if necessary. We are welcomed by loved ones already in spirit and assisted by Transition Guides to reach our higher dimensional destination. The sixth dimension is an ideal destination because our arrival there indicates our evolved nature. Evolution through a successfully completed life, in alignment with our purpose, where we have learned our karmic lessons and expanded as a result. Our purpose is to continually evolve to enable travel through the twelve higher dimensions, on our way back to our real home, where our consciousness originally came from, with our Founder Three Fold Flame[4] Creators, also known as the Cosmic Trinity, or Universal Mind Matrix, in dimensions thirteen, fourteen and fifteen.

Ascension

Self-Realization is our Awakening. We realize the reality of who we are as electrical beings formed from Spirit.

Self-Actualization is our Ascension journey. We acknowledge our potential by restoring our original Divine Eternal Blueprint that was originally created by the Divine Eternal Founder Co-Creator, Three Fold Flame Trinity. While on Earth we seek to unfold through the seven stages as discussed.

Our Evolutionary Journey began when we chose to leave the Monad. We were given a Divine Blueprint in order to have form, and a

Merkeba or Light vehicle in which to travel. We need to keep our Merkeba in good working order. The energy work described in this book will help you do that.

What Is Source Exactly?

Divine God Source Eternal Supreme One is the 'First Cause.' The 'cause' for all that exists as the 'effect.' Source provides Partiki the primal energy units of Ante-Matter as we have discussed. Source is also the Creator of the Twelve Rays.[5]

Divine God Source Eternal Supreme One together with his first creation, the Divine Mother (The Creatrix), have created literally billions of smaller 'Sources', each one with its own 'Co-Creator.' Each Co-Creator embodies a Ray. The Co-Creators and their embodied Rays created the Monadic Vehicle for every human being.

> "In the Beginning was the Void (omnipresent Stillness) and within the Void Divine God Source Eternal Supreme One Spoke the Word (pre-sound vibration) and from the Word came the Light (pre-light oscillation) and from the Light came ALL CREATION"
>
> - FROM THE FREEDOM TEACHINGS BY E'ASHA ASHAYANA

Our Origins

Only a small aspect of our Soul incarnates into our human physical vehicle because the physical body is not large enough to accommodate the whole of the Soul. One Soul can support twelve individual incarnations simultaneously. Added to this, the Soul's home is the Soul plane and therefore the majority of the Soul remains there during our incarnation as 'human.' 'Hu,' by the way, is the Arabic word for 'supreme word.' We were created from sound.

Dimensions

There are twelve dimensions[6] in our Universe. The Third through to sixth dimension is our physical playground.

The Seventh through twelfth dimensions are spiritual realms or cosmic non-physical dimensions, where our higher dimensional selves, souls and monads exist.

Divine God Source Eternal Supreme One level, and the Trinity are outside of space and time in the Trans-Harmonic Universe represented as dimensions thirteen, fourteen and fifteen.

Soul Structures

This information was verbally channeled through the South African channel Theresa Walstra[7] on January 6th, 2018 in reply to my question about the structure of the Soul and Soul Mate relationships. I transcribed it and edited it slightly for ease of reading. The twelve colors spoken of here are not to be taken as meaning the twelve rays specifically. It's analogous.

Soul Structures are difficult to explain because the spirit world works very differently to the material world. This explanation of the structure is a very simplified version and should not be taken literally but used as a working model that will suffice for the purpose of understanding.

Firstly, humans need to stop perceiving themselves as one entity. You are not just a physical body. You are divided into many parts. Emotionally you notice separation into many different parts. You may be aware of a dominant part with peaceful characteristics in addition to an opposite part that may display aggressive tendencies, which may be triggered in certain situations.

Energy is who you are. Unseen but felt. Only the effects can be felt. The energy of electricity cannot be seen but certainly felt if you stick your finger in the electrical socket or get hit by lightning.

Spirit is electrical energy. Your Spirit Self exists in many different planes simultaneously. The Spirit Realm houses a portion of you. There are other portions of you that exist in other realms, in other forms of life outside of your galaxy.

Let's look at Light. Seven colors are a simplification of the frequencies that exist in a rainbow. Many colors make up each color of the rainbow. Many shades.

Your Spirit Self is unified as 'One' in its highest and most expansive form. Eternal Divine Unity is also 'One' – Divine God Source Eternal Supreme One.

Let's say just for the purpose of this explanation that twelve color shades make up a rainbow. Spirit separates into many different 'shades' also. Twelve colors make up the human form. Many billions of colors, many billions of different energies. Do not judge the twelve color choices someone has chosen. They are not representative of the billions that make up the spirit. The twelve suit the path that a soul aspect in incarnation will follow.

If a person chooses the path of a criminal or malicious person, they are not completely evil, their spirit self has simply agreed to incarnate into the form where the human can choose to damage others, or the environment. Before they incarnated they agreed on a spiritual plan which will unfold as they play their part. They have a responsibility to enact what has been agreed in order that they may bring learning to lives of others. All spirit selves therefore benefit.

The most traumatic interactions are the most beneficial to you, if you will but see it. This earthly life is not something that will leave you with scars into eternity. Pain or discomfort may be ultimately beneficial. The twelve colors will translate the learning from earthly experience into the whole of the Spirit structure. This is always change for the better at this level. Your Spirit self is very powerful. It acknowledges that it requires experience, expansion, and energy to grow.

To continue to exist your physical form requires you to ingest nutrients. This concept may be used as a metaphor for Spiritual growth. Experiences and learning are nutrients to be ingested. It's a cyclic process. You may be surprised to learn that there are even nutrients in the air. Tiny types of life forms that are being breathed in. By breathing them in they are destroyed. Converted to another form.

No damage which occurs when in physical form goes to waste, it is all used for the growth of your Spirit Self.

Creator Spirit Beings carefully select which energies need to be incarnated into human, plant, animal, or molecules of air or water.

Let us discuss the Group Spirit. Those who are bound closely, immediate family, the larger family, will, in the Spirit world, exist as a group self. There is also an individual self we may call the Soul Aspect. You, as Soul Aspect, are bonded to others in the group soul while you are on Earth. You are drawn together. You feel you know them even though you just met physically. There is a feeling of familiarity. Karma is best explained by this Group Spirit energy.

Your own choice of twelve color shades, from the billions available, represent your choice of experiences, or the nature of the lives you have chosen to live. This choice, and the motivation behind it, goes well beyond the scope of the understanding available via the current human mind. Soul aspects do not owe anything or have a duty to fulfill anything. It is just that the group made a joint decision about what must be learned by the group as a whole. The incarnated Soul aspect just works towards this communal goal. Your Spirit Self has a natural ability to create expansion.

In meditation you can access more of the colors beyond the twelve.

Hierarchy in spirit exists: you could say as an arrangement of colors. The complexity of physical forms is minor compared to variations in the Spirit world. Spirit Form is very large and complex. It is made up of myriad different energies. There is no human type of emotion in Spirit. Emotions felt whilst in human form do not come close to the feelings that can be felt by your Spirit Self. Those who report the absolute love feelings during a NDE come close. Your physical senses are simply inadequate. You are unable to conceive of the full complexity of it.

Let's make the analogy of a simple single cell organism, the Amoeba, compared to a complex human being. You are like an amoeba when physical, simple, and small, but it is adequate for the earthly journey.

Soul Connections and Twin Flames

Soul connections and Twin Flames are indeed spirit connections. They are examples of the 'recognition of bonding.'

Let's take this further. Bring to mind the rainbow spectrum of color that makes up white. Each color has a different energy/vibration/frequency. Each soul/spirit is made up of vast amounts of energies (like the colors of the spectrum). Only certain colors are required, indeed chosen, for each specific incarnation. Therefore, not all of the colors come to earthly plane, the material world. A great deal of spirit/soul structure remains within the spirit/soul planes.

After Transition the Transition Guide must help to ensure that all the colors of the spectrum, that were present during the earthly incarnation, are moved across to the world of spirit. So called 'hauntings' are caused when some of the colors become 'Earth bound.' When Rita or others do psychic releases on so called 'lost souls' or deceased persons, they are not releasing the entire spectrum of soul aspect energy, they are just releasing a few of the colors that were left behind as it were, a few of the total number that were used for incarnation purposes.

Some people are able to connect with the Spirit world and the Soul structures. Rita is one of them.

In addition to the 'spectrum of colors' the spirit or soul is divided into many different parts.

When you consider so called Twin Flames or Soul Mates you are looking at individuals who are both connected in the spirit world and in present earthly time. In other words, they are connected in another dimension simultaneously to being together on Earth. People become linked together on the earth plane because their souls are drawing them together on the Spirit Plane.

However, your Spirit Selves, your Higher Selves, another portion of your soul or your monad, may also be drawing individuals together from the spirit realms. It is possible that another portion of the soul simultaneously exists in another plane similar to the material plane. There are many planes.

Because of the many realms or dimensions that the complete soul may operate in simultaneously, TIME starts becoming confusing. The individual spectrum frequencies can be active in different places and time is not the same in every place. Some planes operate in non-linear time. In the Spirit world time is of no consequence at all, indeed there is no time. This is because Spirit World is not a plane of material existence. In various planes time does exist, but in different forms.

If you look at the soul, as that encapsulation of the many spectrums, both visible and invisible, each works in a different form. There are many forms. The metaphor of the color spectrum is symbolic of just one form.

In Rita's case there are times when her soul has existed in other realms or dimensions where, it has met and had experiences with her present husband's energy and therefore the energies melded in certain ways. She has also experienced times where she and he formed a group with many others. Also, occurrences where only she formed groups with others. Many existences and many links on many planes.

There are many incarnational opportunities. However, these are not as popularly understood on the earthly plane. Re-incarnation does exist. There is a choice to re-incarnate with other group souls. However, there is often a linking of souls who are drawn together, yet who have not necessarily had specific or direct past life experiences together.

Some might believe that re-incarnation into the Earth plane wastes a great deal of time when they first become aware that there are many other planes where useful experiences may be obtained without so much linear 'time' being spent on those planes. However, all experience is valuable and the choice to incarnate on Earth was made.

Rita's husband, together with a group of others, whom Rita meets sporadically in this life, and also met in other incarnations in different realms, planes and dimensions, are parts of her Group Soul (or more accurately called her 'Team' in Spirit World). This team are constantly being thrown or drawn together, in many incarnations in different planes. This is the same for everyone.

When Regression is experienced by an individual living on the Earth plane often the experiences that become conscious are from the group soul. It should not be understood to be all individual 'past lives' as such, other soul aspects in the group may have had the experiences in their past lives. The healing is for the entire Soul.

Some Soul Aspects become guides to the Aspects incarnated on Earth or elsewhere. Some link only from the point of view that you are group spirit only in the context of this present earthly life.

Imprinting

Imprinting takes place on the earth plane. Humans, plants, and animals leave an imprint of themselves behind when they die. This imprint is held within the Earth Star Chakra, located below the feet within the surface of the Earth.

Through this process of imprinting, incarnated individuals leave behind a gift. Their own most important learnings. People when they die and transition get to choose exactly what they leave behind as their gift to others to come, and to those whom they have both dearly loved and been loved by. This gift may be imprinted on the others that a new incarnating soul aspect is likely to meet.

One of Rita's grandchildren will feel familiar to Rita. This little one holds the imprint of someone Rita has loved before.

This imprinting can be cross gender and cross species. A previously male figure may imprint itself on a freshly incarnating female figure or vice versa. Indeed, a beloved animal like a Cat or a Dog's imprinted gift can become imprinted onto a human.

There is a Spirit Guide Group who is in charge of this 'bestowed gift' process. The Group helps with the scientific operation of this entire process. The soul aspect leaving the physical vehicle as they Transition, interface with this Operator Group in order to have input into the process. The 'gift' may be left in more than one place.

You take with you back to the Spirit plane all the memories of every incident you have experienced while on Earth. Every second is retained as a memory. To begin with the emotions are also retained. Memories, together with emotions, are used by the greater spirit self as lessons to enable expansion. The emotion along with the memory is then discarded when the lesson is learned and fully absorbed by greater spirit self.

When Soul Aspects are planning an incarnation they consider, then choose, the imprinting gifts they deliberately wish to absorb and use for themselves, to aid their Life Purpose or World Service. It is all structured in this way to bring a sense of comfort and connection between people.

Healers generally have a powerful ability to stand alone. They are born to be independent as indeed Rita was. To ensure Healers engage with others for mutual benefit, their Soul ensures the attraction and drawing together of people who need to interact. By engendering a feeling of familiarity, comfort, a sense of belonging or attraction, support is provided as assistance during the process of learning life lessons.

Healers and Spiritual teachers could often easily live alone. However, in that case, they would not experience the earthly incarnation to its fullest. If they were not attracted to others with whom they then develop relationships, they would miss out on many learning opportunities. This methodology ensures camaraderie, togetherness, support, and expansion. Relationships create opportunities for growth.

When plants are harvested as food you do not believe you are destroying life. Think about that. In the same vein you cannot damage your Spirit Self. Its default is to heal and thrive.

Everything is progress. There may be challenge and chaos. The learning is to utilize the energy of turmoil. The Spirit feeds on turmoil, on chaos, as food for growth. This gives access to greater spiritual knowledge. There may be war, conflict, or fighting. There is progress non the less.

It is important that people walk away from hierarchical, and patriarchal, fear-based religions. No true Eternal God is ever destructive, judgmental, or angry at you. Remember you have free will, everything is your choice.

Destiny or Choice

Many people wonder about how much control over their life experiences they have while on Earth. In other words, is there such a thing as Destiny. Is everything set out? Is everything part of a greater plan and as such immutable?

Your full Spirit Self knows what the twelve colors are designated to do during the earthly incarnation. You do, however, have the ability to manifest. You incarnated into a physical body and are just a tiny splinter of what exists in the fullness of your Spirit. You need to interact and relate in order to learn and grow. It's not just about Being, it's about Doing.

It is important that you connect with your Higher Self in order to bring more energy into your life. Striving is important. The choices are yours. The original choices made in the Spirit World may not be recalled by the human personality. However, there is a degree of predictability in human behavior. Let's take the analogy of a tiny child beginning to experience life. It must learn to control bodily functions. It must explore its environment. The sense of taste is valuable in this exploration. The child will put everything in its mouth. That's predictable. A caregiver will simply remove a damaging item. This analogy can be used as an example of predictability; the choices are inevitable. There could have been other choices but the individual was unlikely to make them. Help always comes in times of difficulty because there is a conscious or unconscious request for help.

Remember: Energy cannot be destroyed. It is simply converted. Spirit Self cannot be destroyed therefore your Spirit Self is everlasting.

Theresa's Guides said "This whole subject of Soul Structure, Imprinting, Destiny, Design, Free Will, Incarnation, Re-Incarnation, and Creation, is vastly complex. In its entirety, it is beyond the ability of the human mind, in its present state, to understand. Additionally, the limitedness of the material world poses a barrier to comprehension. Rita's grasp of the subject is now adequate for teaching purposes."

End of channeled material from the Group Cynthia, through Theresa Walstra.

Your Spirit Family Tree

Your Soul can support twelve incarnate beings simultaneously. Your Soul is one of twelve Souls within an Oversoul Structure (aka Monad). Each soul with its twelve maximum incarnate personalities therefore means that a Monad supports a group of up to 144 possible incarnates.

Conclusive Review

Finally let us recap the main points:

- You have a Space of Pure Potential; use it
- Remember the five step SMART plan to aid goal setting
- Remember the Three Pillars concept
- Master your Mind and emotions before they master you
- Honor your Physical body, breathe properly and eat with discernment to keep your gut biome healthy
- Keep your energy flowing
- Choose high vibrational people, places and experiences and work on keeping your own vibration high. Stay away from conflict. Forgive.
- Meditate using the meditations provided or others of equally high vibration, and stay connected to your Higher Self.
- Think and speak avoiding use of the word 'not' so you are congruent instead of conflicted.
- Realize the story you tell yourself about your life is true.
- An attitude of Love and compassion will serve you well
- Avoid why. Use how, what or who, if you want useful answers
- Understand Universal Physics if you want to create miracles in your reality. Remember there are infinite possibilities.
- Manifestation happens when we create a template from scalar waves that then brings our goal into existence.
- It can normally take up to twenty-one days to change the neurological pathways to create a new habit. You naturally receive a new body every seven years. Your stomach lining replaces itself completely every four days. Yet, you can instantly create a new reality when you know how to harness possibilities.
- Focus on expanding your consciousness and increasing your Light Quotient, in order to traverse the Spiritual Unfoldments and connect with your Soul and Monadic self as you move towards Ascension

- Raise your vibration in order to attract high vibrations like abundance consciousness
- Let your Spirit Higher Self as Driver steer your vehicle along its charted course. Relax, trust, and enjoy the view from the passenger seat

What is Fifth Dimensional Consciousness

Many people are aware that Earth and humanity are on their way to changing from a third dimensional reality, to a fifth dimensional reality, by jumping over the fourth dimensional reality. What does that really mean?

According to William Meader, Humanity is now working with the 7th Ray which offers the promise of a new world: a blend of practical with spiritual. We are here to spiritualize form. Ray Seven is anchoring, grounding, and the divine force that gives order to chaos. The urge to organize as a good spiritual quality. The search for right relationship.

In addition, I believe 'living in fifth dimensional consciousness' thereby contributing to ushering in a fifth dimensional reality is founded on:

- An individual aspiration to evolve and increase our light quotient
- Learning how to access our Space of Pure Potential (Higher Heart) and living from there
- Aligning our Hara Lines
- Opening the Green Heart Chakra fully
- Taming the egoic mind
- Acting with love and compassion
- Co-creating a liberated life
- Achieving at least the Third Unfoldment
- Believing in unity (we must stop the erroneous perception of perceived separation and victim/victimizer behaviors or we will exterminate the human race)

If we have embodied the above, we have certainly moved out of third dimensional limitedness. We have stopped being cognitively blind to anything outside of the third dimensional matrix. Therefore, with every additional person who awakens and is able to 'live in the fifth', we will be one step closer to having ushered in the ascension timeline, of a fifth dimensional earth plane, founded on Love, Freedom and Unity. In Philosophy the concept of Downward Causation[8] says there is a causal relationship from higher levels of a system to lower levels. All processes at the lower level of a hierarchy are restrained by, and act in conformity to the higher level. For example, if 1% of molecules in a system rise to a higher frequency and become coherent, they can then transform the remaining low frequency, or chaotic 99%, into coherence. Therefore 1% of humanity embodying fifth dimensional consciousness can usher the remaining 99% into the Fifth Dimensional, Divinely Decreed, Evolved New World, of Unity, Equality, Freedom and Love.

NOTES

Chapter One – Finding Truth

1. Neuro-linguistic programming (NLP) is an approach to communication, personal development, and psychotherapy created by Richard Bandler and John Grinder in California, United States in the 1970s.

2. Metaphysical refers to beyond physical

3. Cymatics, from Greek meaning "wave", is a subset of modal vibrational phenomena. The term was coined by Hans Jenny (1904-1972), a Swiss follower of the philosophical school known as anthroposophy. Typically the surface of a plate, diaphragm or membrane is vibrated, and regions of maximum and minimum displacement are made visible in a thin coating of particles, paste or liquid. Different patterns emerge in the excitatory medium depending on the geometry of the plate and the driving frequency. Read more in Glossary section.

4. The Three Laws have been expressed in several different ways and can be summarized as follows. The First Law says an object either remains at rest or continues to move at a constant velocity unless acted upon by an external force. The Second law says the vector sum of the forces on an object is equal to the mass of that object multiplied by the acceleration vector of the object. (Vector definition in mafirstths and physics: a numerical value in a specific direction. You need both value and direction to have a vector). The Third Law says that when one body exerts a force on a second body, the second body simultaneously exerts a force equal in magnitude and opposite in direction on the first body. Force can be seen at work when two billiard balls collide.

5. Nuclear Engineer, Lt Colonel Thomas E Bearden Retired PhD,MS (Nuclear engineering), BS (mathematics and minor electrical engineering) Co-Inventor of the 2002 Motionless Electronic generator, and more commonly known in his field as Tom Bearden

6. http://docplayer.net/1426756-Rapid-and-decisive-solution-of-the-world-energy-crisis-and-global-warming.html

7. Richard P. Feynman (1918-1988), scientist, teacher, raconteur, and musician assisted in the development of the atomic bomb, expanded the understanding of quantum electrodynamics, translated Mayan hieroglyphics, and cut to the heart of the Challenger disaster. However, beyond all of that, Richard Feynman was a unique and multi-faceted individual.

8. <u>Bruce H. Lipton, The Biology of Belief: Unleashing the Power of Consciousness, Matter and Miracles</u>

9. It's worth noting here that there have been three major 'falls' of man. The original downfall, which became known as 'original sin', occurred some 550 million years ago. The second fall, was 5.5 million years ago. In addition, there was the Luciferic Rebellion in 25,500 BC. 'Luciferic' could be said to depict the distortions in consciousness arising from excess masculine energy. Long story short the Luciferic Rebellion resulted in our Merkabas changing spin into reverse. This gave rise, to shadow selves being created. Severe DNA mutations of life forms on Earth have been the result of this tampering.

10. Milton Erickson (deceased) was considered by some to be the greatest Hypnotherapist of all time. Certainly ahead of his time.

11. Prime Directives means main responsibilities or 'hard wired' to carry out those responsibilities.

12. Carl Gustav Jung 1875-1961 was a Swiss psychiatrist and psychoanalyst who founded analytical psychology.

13. See Glossary and associated chapter for definition

14. The Orgone Accumulator Handbook: Natural Energy Works, Ashland, Oregon 2010

15. According to Carl G. Jung: On the nature of the Psyche

16. Jon Rappoport was a candidate for a US Congressional Seat in the 29th District of California. Nominated for a Pulitzer Prize. He helps people expand their personal creative power. Book: *Power outside the Matrix* http://marketplace.mybigcommerce.com/power-outside-the-matrix/

Chapter Two – Finding the Science, the Sacred Geometry

1. Dr. Walter Bowman Russell (May 19, 1871 – May 19, 1963) was an impressionist American painter (of the Boston School), sculptor, natural philosopher, musician, author, and builder. The New York Herald Tribune called him "the modern Leonardo",[1] a Renaissance man for the twentieth century. Although considered by some a polymath, Russell was not an academician. He has left a legacy that centers around his unique Cosmogony, or concept of the universe, having spent many years writing about the nature of humankind's relationship to the Universal One and the degrees of consciousness. His work appeals to those who are not only seekers but scientist, or those where that division ceases to exist. https://youtu.be/YRX_fMDkxTo

2. Robert Otey and Matt Presti video production https://youtu.be/x4LFPiuRfp4

2. Edward N Lorenz (1917 – 2008) an American mathematician, meteorologist, and a pioneer of

chaos theory.

3. The Vocation of Man (1800) **Johann Gottlieb Fichte** (1762 –1814) German philosopher

4. I include this section with grateful thanks to my dear friend and color therapist Tanya Lee Collop https://www.tanyaleecollop.co.za.

Chapter Three – Finding Systems

1. You Tube Video Inner Life of a cell http://multimedia.mcb.harvard.edu/ https://youtu.be/yKW4F0Nu-UY

2. The hundredth monkey effect is a phenomenon in which a new behavior or idea is spread rapidly through the morphic field from one group to all related groups once a critical number of members of one group exhibit the new behavior or acknowledge the new idea. This phenomenon was mentioned by Lyall Watson (1938-2008) in his book *Lifetide* (1979), who documents the case with references to five highly respectable articles by Japanese primatologists (Imanishi 1963; Kawai 1963 and 1965; Kawamura 1963; and Tsumori 1967).

3. Free book download http://free-ebooksdownloadhelper.blogspot.co.za/2014/02/the-hidden-messages-in-water-by-masaru.html

4. Editorial Review: The Hidden Messages in Water is impressive. Through his genius photography and very good scientific talent, Dr. Masaru Emoto has created a book that's actually a mystical treasure. His contribution to analysis in religious consciousness is completely masterful. Caroline M. Myss, author of *Sacred Contracts and Anatomy of the Spirit*

5. Read more about holograms in this context: Brain and Perception: Holonomy and Structure in Figural Processing Karl H Pribram

6. Just in case you are unfamiliar with who Tesla (1856-1943) was: Vice President Behrend of the Institute of Electrical Engineers in his speech when presenting Tesla with the Edison medal, eloquently expressed the following: "Were we to seize and eliminate from our industrial world the result of Mr. Tesla's work, the wheels of industry would cease to turn, our electric cars and trains would stop, our towns would be dark and our mills would be idle and dead. His name marks an epoch in the advance of electrical science."

7. https://www.youtube.com/watch?v=7VINZ0P-Ay0 Meyl's equipment demonstrated

8. Partiki is a term from Keylonta Science by A Deane

9. Terminology from *Voyagers The Secret of Amenti, Volume II* about Keylonta Science by A Deane

10. Interested in reading more? The book *Zero: The Biography of a Dangerous Idea* by Charles Seife.

"Charles Seife has made a marvelously entertaining something out of nothing. By simply telling the tale of zero, Seife provides a fresh and fascinating history not only of mathematics but also of science, philosophy, theology, and even art. An impressive debut for a promising young science writer." –John Horgan.

11. (sacred) knowledge

12. Fuller description of holograms http://www.explainthatstuff.com/holograms.html

13. Repeating.

14. Thanks to http://pages.cs.wisc.edu/~ergreen/honors_thesis/ani_snowflake.html for image

Chapter Four – Finding Health

1. Page 31 of Aura Soma Healing Through Color, Plant and Crystal Energy by Irene Dalichow and Mike Booth

2. https://www.ted.com/talks/brene_brown_on_vulnerability#t-4908

3. Shtetl: a self-sufficient little community or town. People each doing their own piece within the whole. Origin: yiddish.

4. Philanthropist: The word comes from the Greek philanthro meaning towards and philanthrópía which means love for mankind so a philanthropist is one who moves towards love for mankind.

Chapter Five – Finding Who You Really Are

1. Merkeba is a moving Light Body. A set of counter-rotating, electro-magnetic energy spirals.

2. http://www.janegoodall.ca/goodall-bio-timeline.php

3. The Merchant of Venice, Act IV, Scene I

4. See section on Unfoldments for more detail

5. Espirit de corps: a feeling of pride and mutual loyalty shared by group members

6. Monad is the Soul's Soul.

Chapter Six – Finding Love

1. Itzhak Bentov (1923-1979) was a scientist, engineer, inventor, and an early pioneer in the research of consciousness. By blending analytical knowledge and intuitive insight, Bentov was the first to develop what is now widely accepted today as a holographic model of reality. He wrote widely on the mechanics of consciousness.

2. From Atom to Cosmos video https://youtu.be/KMbeK_6ATxQ

3. Archons for definition see Glossary

4. Bucharest Early Intervention Project (BEIP) headed by neurologist Charles Nelson of Harvard Medical School, was spurred to action by the collapse of Romania's Nicolae Ceaucescu regime in 1989, which had shunted tens of thousands of unwanted children into state-run orphanages.

5. Thomas Warren Campbell (Dec 9 1944) is a physicist, lecturer and author of the *My Big T.O.E.* (Theory of everything) trilogy, a work that claims to unify general relativity, quantum mechanics and metaphysics along with the origins of consciousness.

6. Read the section What is Source for more detail

7. Sir David Ramon Hawkins, M.D, Ph.D was a nationally renowned psychiatrist, physician, researcher, spiritual teacher and lecturer. The uniqueness of his contribution to humanity comes from the advanced state of spiritual awareness known as Enlightenment or Self–Realization he attained. Rarely, if ever, has this spiritual state occurred in the life of an accomplished scientist and physician. Therefore, Dr. Hawkins was uniquely qualified to present a spiritual path that is scientifically compelling to modern society.

Chapter Seven – Finding Guidance

1. https://www.iarc.fr/en/media-centre/iarcnews/pdf/MonographVolume112.pdf

2. These seven major unfoldments were delineated clearly in the Theosophical Society, headed by Madame Blavatsky, and in the Alice Bailey books written by the Ascended Master Djwhal Khul.

3. In psychological terms the Light can be viewed as the most advanced and "higher minded" portions of our consciousness that lead us toward enlightenment. In energetic terms Light stands for the portions of our psyche that vibrate the highest, the highest frequency parts of our energy-identity, such as the Super-conscious Mind, the Higher Self and the Soul. In terms of our collective psyche, the Light represents the people that hold the highest frequency awareness and most expanded consciousness, who serve as a force of evolution toward enlightenment, expression and empowerment for the masses. Thanks to http://www.ascensiondictionary.com/2017/07/light-and-shadow.html for definition.

4. For definition of Three Fold Flame see Glossary

5. Alice Bailey, *Esoteric Healing Vol IV A Treatise on the Seven Rays,* Lucis Publishing ISBN 0853301212

6. Dimensions are fixed groupings of energy within specific geometric arranged forms (space and time) and are built upon crystallized conscious units of sound and light called Morphogenetic Fields. Using the instruction sets from Morphogenetic Fields, dimensions are composed of

stationary points of the vibration of sound and light, which together form a fabric of tone and into which smaller morphogenetic fields are woven. From each fixed point of sound vibration and within each dimension of manifestation field, an electrical current of Consciousness emerges. There is layer upon layer upon layer of morphogenetic fields and dimensional reality systems. A dimension is a full frequency band: repeating sequences of waves flashing on and off (particle/anti-particle universe) and it's what we're existing in space with. "Dimensions" are a means of organizing different planes of existence according to their vibratory rate. Each dimension has certain sets of laws and principles that are specific to the frequency of that dimension. "Consciousness" represents awareness. The inhabitants of each dimension function clearly, easily, and with a minimum of resistance within that plane because their consciousness vibrates in resonance with the frequency of that dimension.

"Multidimensional Consciousness" is the ability to be "conscious" of more than one dimension. To be multidimensional in our consciousness we must remember that we have within us the potential to expand our perceptual awareness to the dimensions above and below our physical plane. Thanks to https://ascensionglossary.com/index.php/Dimensions

7. theresa@theresawalstra.com
8. Donald T. Campbell defined Downward Causation in 1974 as all processes at the lower level of a hierarchy are restrained by and act in conformity to the laws of the higher level

Glossary

1. Partiki is a term from Keylonta Science translated from the CDT Plates by Ashayana Deane

GLOSSARY

Term	AKA in other systems	Function or meaning
Akashic Records	CDT Plates	Akasha: An etheric record of the experiences of the Earth and each incarnated being. Like an etheric computer holographic hard drive with lots of files. The CDT Plates are 12 actual silver-alloy discs that contain, in holographic format within striated-selenite-quartz crystal, the true history of the Earth and her peoples from 950 billion years ago. They are both recording, storage and transmission devices in scalar wave form, which are translated by nominated CDT Plate Speakers.
Archons	Negative Artificial Intelligence	A False King of Tyranny Ruler that has greed for domination. Who controls through masks of deception promoted through warring technological abuse, such as mind control, frequency implants, and military strategies. The Archontic Deception and its Patriarchal Oligarchy stems mostly from the Draconian races from the Orion Constellation aka the Orion Group.
Awareness	Mindfulness	A way of being where there is an ability to be an objective observer of one's life.

Birth into Matter		Physical birth. We had infinite awareness at birth (extreme psychic ability) we lose it as we grow more and more familiar with the earth plane. By the age of seven most people have lost psychic ability and awareness of metaphysical realms. We can work to recover our abilities.
Birth into Spirit		Death. Transition out of planes of matter into planes of Spirit
Calibrate		To calibrate is to measure. A standard scale used for comparison to check accuracy of function. Calibration is an adjustment to improve function.
Causations Origins	NLP teaches: C > E Cause is greater than effect. Get to cause and you can easily change	Root cause of a problem/ issue / perception. Origin is a better word than causality because causality is in the mind not in the world. Potentiality becomes an actuality. An origin can be a multiple of things. Info brought in with you. Promises made etc. A causation is a specific event. An insult of some kind.
Cosmic Day		There is a Cosmic Day and a Cosmic Night. Cosmic versions of our Earth day (expansion) and night (rest). A cosmic day is said to last 4.3 billion years. Within the Cosmic days and nights Eternal Source breathes in or out approximately every thirteen thousand years. A complete breath every 26,000 years. The last mid-point between the breaths occurred in 2012. The

		Mayan Calendar recorded this event. The mid-point of Source breathing has the same potential as the midpoint of the human breath we term the Moment of Suspension or Zero - Point in this book.
Cosmic Egg		According to Itzak Bentov the first separation, a division to create a mated pair, that began the whole of existence. An excellent animation can be found here https://youtu.be/pPhfA9N2uMg
Cymatics		Sound made visible. Cymatics, from Greek meaning "wave", is a subset of modal vibrational phenomena. The term was coined by Hans Jenny (1904-1972), a Swiss follower of the philosophical school known as Anthroposophy. Typically, the surface of a plate, diaphragm or membrane is vibrated, and regions of maximum and minimum displacement are made visible in a thin coating of particles, paste or liquid. Different patterns emerge in the excitatory medium depending on the geometry of the plate and the driving frequency. On July 8, 1680, Robert Hooke was able to see the nodal patterns associated with the modes of vibration of glass plates. Hooke ran a violin bow along the edge of a glass plate covered with flour, and saw the nodal patterns emerge
Dark Matter	Anti-matter	The other side of the mirror from Earth/humanity. Correspondingly Earth/humanity represents

		the dark side to others not of the earth plane.
Divine Creative Intent	Eternal Source, Creator, the All That is, Prima Materia, Divine architect, God	First Cause, Divine Unity, Divine God Source Eternal Supreme One
Energetic Precedence		Energy field around each person that is much bigger than just the aura.
Fractal	As above, so below	All energy is fractal in nature. A copy of a pattern. A repeat of a repeat of a repeat of a pattern. In a Fractal the smallest portion is repetitive to the grandest portion - all places of a fractal are connected. A snowflake is a good example of a fractal. A fractal is a good example of a repetitive system.
Hara Center	Tan Tien	A sphere one inch in diameter located below the navel behind the sacral chakra where the figure of eight energetic flow crosses over. Our reservoir of original energy created when sperm and ovum created zygote. Two polarities came together as one. The Monad seats itself here. The Tan Tien envelops the Hara Center in a soccer ball size bubble of energy.
Hara Dimension		The Hara Dimension is a meta program from which creation happens. Enormous creative power resides here.

Hara Lines Hara Line Main Central Channel	Sushumna	The Seven Keys to Health are the 7 hara lines. They are affected by insults in that they can misalign, become un-set, occlude, truncate, disconnect, become split etc. They are multidimensional in nature. Each has an associated color frequency. 1 & 2: Black & White - connections to Now and Will (aka Ida and Pinglali Nadi) 3: Green – Navigation 4: Yellow to Red – Receiving 5: Blue - Life Purpose 6 & 7: The sexuality lines. 6 is Resilience and female. 7 is Strength and Energy and male. Pink and Magenta respectively
Higher Self		Neither spirit nor matter but the relation between the two. The connection between Monad, Soul, and incarnated personality. The Mediator or Middle Principle. Only present during incarnation. The force of evolution itself. The constructor of forms. The co-creative agent. The plural term Higher Selves may be used as a collective noun for the Higher Self connection, Soul, Monad, and higher dimensional selves. There are 3D, 4D, 5D, 6D, 7D, 8D, 9D, 10D, 11D, and 12th Dimensional selves.
Human Primary Directive		To live, learn and grow. Problems arise when one or more of these are neglected
Insult	Limiting decisions	Shocks or traumas that affect the nervous system physically, emotionally, or mentally. Abuse, neglect, industrial chemical

	Limiting Beliefs Parts Soul fragmentation	poisons, poor quality water, air pollution, are all insults that affect health and well-being. Insults can affect the child in utero. Lower vibrational experiences. Anything that destructs the healthy normal function of a system (system being cell to planet - size irrelevant).
Kryst	Christ Krystos Chryst	We aim to stand in the Kryst. Kryst is a word that expresses the first audible sound tones that preceded Creation. The love principle. The change of spelling occurred when the sound Kryst was written in English.
Laws	Universal Laws	Advice on how to live optimally
Metaphysical		Beyond physical. Beyond the awareness of our five physical senses. Metaphysical phenomena is perceived by our Higher Sensory Perception, our awareness, our intuition. Our claircognizance (knowing), clairaudience (hearing), clairsentience (feeling), clairvoyance (seeing). Our senses only detect effect. The cause is often metaphysical. Empirical knowledge is invalid because it relies only on the senses and ignores metaphysical cause. True knowledge is the understanding of the cause.
Mind		The thinking authority and inner awareness for this incarnation.
Mis-perception/ mis-apprehension/ mis-alignment		Perception is projection. Things that are coming at you are coming from you. Stop putting the

		responsibility outside oneself. Stop transference of one's own issues onto others. We catch misapprehensions like diseases.
Moment of Being		The shift from spirit to flesh. Moment of creation of the Template. Sometimes a person chooses a Divine Perfection Template others chose a flawed template if it suits their needs for the incarnation. Flawed templates may be exchanged during life, on demand, if it's beneficial and the associated lessons have been learned. Life choices may mean the original template becomes redundant and therefore requires replacing.
Monad	Oversoul	Our Soul's Soul. The immortal essence of ourselves which uses the soul to incarnate through, just as the soul incarnates through our personality. Aka our I Am Presence. Or as we prefer our 'We Are Presence' Monad means one or unity. It remains unrevealed until after the third unfoldment. Building of the bridge between lower and higher mind is the first step towards achieving monadic consciousness, and thus the first step towards the Way of Higher Evolution. The Monad seats itself in the Hara Center during an incarnation.
Origin		See Causation
Partiki	God Particle	The Scalar Waves are created from the smallest units of consciousness called Partiki.[1] You could say the Partiki is the much sought after 'God Particle.' It is

		the first act of creation from our Divine God Source Eternal Supreme One and separates into Partika and Particum
Particum Partika		Partiki as pre-matter (ante-matter) have the ability to create both matter and its opposite, anti-matter. Partiki split into two polarities or fields in the act of fission. On one side Particum create the Universe where we have our existence. On the other side Partika give rise to the anti-matter universe. Partika and Particum are the building blocks of creation.
Perception	Issue Problem Model of the World (NLP) Internal representation Insisted on Stories	Perception comes via observation/experience/ information. How we process our experiences based on the Filters (like a selective camera lens) we develop at an unconscious mind level through life experience and/or insults. Humans are altered by their environment. Our model of the world is based on perceptions (accurate or inaccurate). We are a biological computer. The software develops over time. The hardware is donated by Spirit through a combining of spirit and matter. Perceptions can be controlled and/or influenced by outside forces such as government, church, military, family, tribe, culture, educators, media, peers, manipulators.
Perception is projection	The Law of Return	Things that are coming at you are coming from you. Your reality is observer-created.

Pivot Point	In NLP called a reframe or belief change	A change occurring quickly as a result of an experience. To pivot in mind is the same as to pivot in dancing. To change direction. To consciously change a habitual thought process. To deliberately choose a new thought that is in vibrational harmony with a new desire. As in, the experience was pivotal in my life.
Self-organizing		Is a process whereby an overall order appears from specific interactions between individual parts of an initially disordered system. The process is spontaneous and happens without control from an external force, the system inherently knows how to create order from chaos.
Soul		Essentially it is Light, both literally from the vibratory angle, and symbolically, for it is like the rays of the sun, which pour out into the darkness. The way of the incarnate human being becomes increasingly illumined. Spirit and matter, when brought into a close rapport, necessarily exert an effect upon each other. Matter, is spiritualized. The Soul is one of the twelve progeny of the Monad.
Soul Mates		See Twin Flames
Spirit		Spirit as verb: the central electrical energy which is the cause of all manifestation; the word spirit is applied to that undefinable, elusive, essential impulse or Life which is the cause of all

		manifestation; the breath of Life; spirit is matter at its highest point of expression, and matter is spirit at its lowest. Spirit as noun can refer to the non-physical realms and the beings who inhabit those realms.
Surrender		Yield. Release. Let go of. Open to.
System		Systems are all there is. Everything is a part of one.
Syntocracy		A Syntocracy is a system where each member is honored as equal and where each contributes equally to the success of the system. As may be observed in a beehive.
The battle		Perceived separation. We must stop this erroneous perception or exterminate ourselves.
The Word		See vibration and Kryst
Three Fold Founder Flame	Universal Trinity Rishi Matrix	Blue Flame of the Divine Mother in 13D. Violet-Magenta flame of the Divine Father in 15D. Golden Yellow Ray Sun of Christos in 14D. Together they make up the Trinity that created our entire Universal Time Matrix.
Torus	Toroid	Tonal resonators within male and female electrical vortices
Twelve Rays		The twelve qualities of light (divine manifestation) that Eternal Source uses to create everything that exists. Our Monads are directly associated with a specific ray which enables us to embody the qualities of the ray.

The first seven rays are called
Ray One Divine Will & Power or
the Lightning which annihilates
Ray Two Love & Wisdom or the
Cosmic Magnet
Ray Three Active Intelligence or
the Keeper of the Records
Ray Four Harmony Through
Conflict or the Seed that is the
Flower
Ray Five Pure Intelligence and
Concrete Knowledge or the Dis-
penser of Knowledge
Ray Six Idealism & Devotion or
the Negator of Desire
Ray Seven Gateway to a New
Age and Ceremonial Order or
the Keeper of the Magical Word.
For more info, read Alice Bailey
*Esoteric Healing Vol IV A Trea-
tise on the Seven Rays* Lucis
Publishing ISBN 0853301212.
Ray 8 Cleansing
Ray 9 Loosening ties to physical
plane and establishing contact
with Soul.
Ray 10 is the Body of Light
Ray 11 Bridge to a New Age
Ray 12 The New Age: combines
all 12 Rays in gold.
According to William Meader
Earth has 3rd ray personality,
2nd ray soul, and 1st ray monad.
Humanity is now working with
the 7th Ray which offers the
promise of a new world: a blend
of practical with spiritual. We are
here to spiritualize form. Ray 7 is
anchoring and grounding & the
divine force that gives order to
chaos. The urge to organize as a
good spiritual quality. The
Search for right relationship: between nations/religions/money/
humanity's crisis.

		Grounding mystical ideas. Together with Ray Five, my Monad's ray, it inspired this book.
Twin Flames		A soul is able to send aspects of itself into 12 simultaneous incarnations. 6 pairs of male and female. This pairing is known as 'Twin Flames.' Slightly different to Soul Mates which are not paired but one of the 12. Twin flames may never meet on the earth plane. If they do, there may, or may not be, a romantic attraction.
Vibration Is a continuum depending on the point from which you perceive it. Everything reduces to vibration		Everything that exists has a unique vibration. Animals, birds, humans, bacteria, plants, the Sun, rocks, crystals. Human emotions each carry a vibration. Like attracts like. The vibration of the human dictates the level of health. The language of the living energy codes of matter, which is made of light, sound, frequency and vibration Vibration (energy contracts towards the neutral point) leads to oscillation (moving away from a neutral point), leads to vibrational frequency rate. Frequency meaning how often a wave passes a fixed point.
Wisdom	Intuition Higher Self guidance Knowledge of and	Wisdom is knowing how little we know. Cleverness without wisdom is the most destructive force on Earth. Wisdom is gained not taught.

	adherence to Divine Truth	
Zero Point Sphere	Vertex Singularity are used in the context of toroidal vortex model	Spiral Vortex Model: According to Russellian Science the sphere created at the center of the union of two spiral electrical generator male and female vortices where infinite possibilities are accessible via Scalar wave grids. Omnipresent stillness. A neutral place. The core light that emanates from the zero point sphere is the Divine Light that created all things.

BIBLIOGRAPHY

A. Parthasarathy *Vedanta Treatise* Vedanta Life Institute India
www.vedanta-edu.org

AArt Jurriaanse *Bridges* `Sun Centre' School of Esoteric Philosophy
South Africa ISBN 103929345110

Gary M Douglas Dain Heer *The Home of Infinite Possibilities* Access
Consciousness Publishing ISBN978-1634931281

Alan Jacobs *The Gnostic Gospels* Watkins Publishing London ISBN
9781842930991

Alan W. Watts *The Book on the Taboo Against Knowing Who You Are*
Collier Books 8th printing 1969 LCCCN66-10408

Alice Bailey *Esoteric Healing Vol IV* A Treatise on the Seven Rays Lucis
Publishing ISBN 0853301212

Anneliese Cowley founder St Francis Health Centre Port Alfred South
Africa for sharing her personal teachings with me and facilitating my
health and personal growth during my many stays at her health centre

Ann Hill A Visual Encyclopedia of Unconventional Medicine New
English Library ISBN 450044475

Ashayana Deane *Voyager Series The Secrets of Amenti Reprised 2017*
ARhAyas Productions ISBN978069284552-3

Dr. Carl Johan Calleman and Ian Xel Lungold for their teachings on
the Mayan Calendar

Barbara Ann Brennan *Hands of Light* Bantam Books ISBN
0553345397

Barbara Ann Brennan *Light Emerging* Bantam Books ISBN
0553354566

Bruce Lipton *The Biology of Belief* Mountain of Love/Elite Books
0975991477

C W Leadbeatter *The Chakras* Theosophical Publishing House ISBN 0835604225

Caroline Myss *Sacred Contracts* Bantam Books ISBN

Caroline Myss with Norman Shealy MD *Why people don't heal and how they can* Bantam Books ISBN 9780553814941

Charles Seife *The biography of a dangerous idea. The tale of zero.* Penguin ISBN 978-0140296471

Coby Zvickler *The Key To Gabriel* Gabriel Publications ISBN 0953511502

David V Tansley DC *Radionics and the Subtle Anatomy of Man* Health Science Press ISBN 0850320895

Deb Shapiro *Your Body Speaks your mind* Piatkus ISBN 9780749927837

Deepak Chopra *Life after Death* Harmony Publishing 978-1400052356

Diane Stein *All Women are Healers* Crossing Press ISBN 089594409X

Diane Stein *Essential Energy Balancing* Crossing Press ISBN 9781580910286

Diane Stein *Psychic Healing with Spirit Guides and Angels* Crossing Press ISBN 0895948079

Don Greeenbank *A Healers Pathway* Regency Press ISBN 0721208134

Dr. David Hawkins *Transcending the Levels of Consciousness* Veritas Publishing ISBN 0971500746

Eileen Hutchins *Parzival* Temple Lodge Publishing ISBN 9781906999353

Florence Shovel Shinn *The Power of the Spoken Word* LN Fowler & Co UK 1959 ISBN not allocated 85243.089 2

Hulda Regehr Clark PhD., N.D. *The Cure for All Diseases* New Century Press ISBN 1890035017

Irene Dalichow & Mike Booth *Aura Soma Healing Through Color*, Plant and Crystal Energy, Hayhouse ISBN 1561703222

Itzhak Bentov *A Brief Tour of Higher Consciousness: A Cosmic Book on the Mechanics of creation* Destiny Books; 2nd Edition, Revised Edition of *A Cosmic Book* edition (April 1 2000) ISBN978-0892818143

Jack Temple *Medicine Man* Findhorn Press ISBN 1899171495

James Redfield *The Celestine Prophecy* ISBN 1594831955

Jane Roberts *The Seth Material* Prentice Hall Inc. ISBN 0138071985

Lao Tzu *Tao Te Ching* Watkins London ISBN 9781842930564

Leslie Temple-Thurston *The Marriage of Spirit* Core Light Publishing ISBN 1931679053

Lt Colonel Thomas E Bearden Retired PhD,MS Nuclear Engineer aka Tom Bearden Co-Inventor of the 2002 Motionless Electronic generator, has done some sterling work which is useful in understanding how we can have energy that does not involve raping the planet, mining coal, drilling or fracking for oil, drilling for gas and creating an ecological disaster in the process.
http://docplayer.net/1426756-Rapid-and-decisive-solution-of-the-world-energy-crisis-and-global-warming.html

Lynne McTaggart *The Field* Harper Perennial 978-0061435188

Margaret Roberts *Tissue Salts for Healthy Living* Penguin Random House ISBN 9781770077737

Masuro Emoto *The Hidden Messages in Water* Simon & Schuster UL Limited ISBN1416522190

Melody *Love is in the Earth* Properties of the Mineral Kingdom Earth-Love Publishing ISBN 0962819034

Michael Talbot *The Holographic Universe* Harper Collins ISBN 0586091718

Mouni Sadhu *Samadhi* George Allen & Unwin Ltd ISBN 004149006

Nikola Tesla *The Inventions Researches and Writings of Nikola Tesla* by Thomas Commerford Martin Published in the *Electrical Engineer* 1894 republished by Health Research PO Box 70 Mokelumne Hill California 95245 in 1970

Orin and DaBen Sanaya Roman & Duane Packer *Awakening Your Light Body* LuminEssence Productions Oakland CA

Orin and DaBen Sanaya Roman and Duane Packer *Becoming Radiant* LuminEssence Productions Oakland CA

Paramhansa Yoganada *Autobiography of a Yogi* Rider & Company ISBN 0090210530

Paul Foster Case *The Tarot Key to the Wisdom of the Ages* Builders of the Adytum ISBN 0938002082

Ra Uru Hu & Lynda Bunnell *Human Design The Science of Differentiation* HDC Publishing ISBN9780615552149

Dr. Rashid Buttar DO, FAAPM, FACAM, FAAIM, Center for Advanced Medicine

Richard Feynman lectures http://www.feynmanlectures.caltech.edu/

Richard Gerber MD *Vibrational Medicine for the 21st Century* Piatkus ISBN 0749921188

Robert Otey *Gravity is a Myth* available from his website www.feandft.com

Rudolph Steiner *How to Know Higher Worlds* Anthroposophic Press ISBN 0880103728

Sandy Stevenson *The Awakener* Gateway Books ISBN 1858600405

Sogyal Rinpoche *The Tibetan Book of Living and Dying* Rider Random House ISBN 0712657525

Swami Muktananda Kundalini *The Secret of Life* Siddha Yoga Publication ISBN0911307346

Taoist Master Alfred Huang *The Complete I Ching* Inner Traditions ISBN 0892816562

Tom Campbell *My Big TOE* A Trilogy Unifying Philosophy, Physics, and Metaphysics ISBN: 0-972509402

Victor E. Frankl *Mans Search For Meaning* ISBN 9781846041242

Virginia Essene *Channelled New Teachings for Awakening* Humanity ISBN 0937147001

Walter Russell for his *Russellian Science* and his legacy of the University of Science and Philosophy https://www.philosophy.org

William Meader Emergent Light https://meader.org

INDEX

ABOUT THE AUTHOR

I was a casualty of the Gulf War in 1991 together with my business and its 160 employees. The total loss of everything, house, car, business, future security, caused me to re-assess my life, I woke up, connected to my Higher Self, then went about discovering my life purpose. I spent years on self-healing, personal growth, and re-training for my second career which was helping others as a Spiritual Psychotherapist, Energy Healer and Teacher of Metaphysics. I know now that my Soul's guidance has been invaluable in making the years since 1991 fulfilling and successful.

I became known as the 'Light-worker's Light-worker' as many of my clients were therapists and light-workers who needed someone with a higher vibration than their own to assist them evolve and heal.

I grappled with Quantum Physics and the concept that the observer affects the observed. I came to fully appreciate the Universal Laws. I successfully mastered the power of intention and began to grasp the nature of the Morphogenetic Field that connects us all. I discovered the importance of Hara Lines, Toroids and Spiral Vortices, and my work rose to another level.

In March 2016 I received an email from Sally Reid, then unknown to me, who asked to make an appointment for a Haric Alignment. During the first five minutes of the VOIP call we both felt there was a bigger reason for our meeting than just an alignment. Sally, who is a Medical Intuitive and a clear channel for Spirit heard a message spontaneously come through for me. She suddenly said, "My Guides say they have information for you that will enhance your understanding of the Hara Lines, eventually you will write a book to disseminate this information." We were both shocked. Then I recalled that a Psychic had said to me when I was in my twenties, 'you will write a book.' I had written many student manuals and blogs over the years. Many people had asked 'when are you going to write a book?' but I never felt the impulse. Suddenly the best opportunity in the world was being offered to me. How could I do anything but embrace the chance to fulfil my purpose at the next level?

We had both been picked to fulfil a mission. The Council of Truth had been consistently sharing their knowledge for thousands of years and finally it was our turn to be the messengers. Sally is a clear channel and I used my scribing skills to take the channeled words and mold them into a clear and readable format that is easy to teach and understand. My Certified Trainer of NLP skills came in very handy. I was able to ground the information. I am delighted to have been able to fulfil my spiritual calling in a such an aligned way. I owe deep gratitude for everything I share with you to The Council of Truth and Sally for being their mouthpiece.

As I look back over my life, I wouldn't change a thing. All the trials and tribulations were learning opportunities where I was guided by my Soul, given the 'Divine Nudge' you might say, to get back onto the path I had chosen to tread in my earthly life. Sometimes if we are going in the wrong direction Spirit finds a way to place a hurdle before us so that in our quest to get around it we find a whole new route opening up. A route that is easier and more suited to who we are.

Over twenty-five years of study and practice enabled me to pick out the ritual from the recipe book and be left with simply what works. Ritual, drama, fasting, and time-consuming expensive disciplines, were devised to give a sense of mystery to what is basically just a matter of finding what works. You will find all mythology stripped from my methods. I focus only on truth and health and 'all is energy' is truth.

Jim Carey once said when addressing graduation students "Our need for acceptance can make us invisible in this world. Risk being seen in all of your glory." I am here, risking all, to share with you information which I truly hope will be life changing enough for you to want to share with others.

I believe the only limits we have, are the ones we create. That being the case we can choose to un-create them and be limitless.

Made in the USA
Monee, IL
19 March 2021

63159721R00154